GRIEZMANN

MATT AND TOM OLDFIELD

ULTIMATE
FOOTBALL HEROES

GRIEZMANN

FROM THE PLAYGROUND
TO THE PITCH

DINO

Published by Dino Books,
an imprint of John Blake Publishing,
The Plaza,
535 Kings Road,
Chelsea Harbour,
London SW10 0SZ

www.johnblakepublishing.com

www.facebook.com/johnblakebooks
twitter.com/jblakebooks

First published in paperback in 2019

ISBN: 978 1 78946 113 8

British Library Cataloguing-in-Publication Data:

A catalogue record for this book is available from the British Library.

Design by www.envydesign.co.uk

Printed and bound in Great Britain by Clays Ltd, Elcograf S.p.A.

1 3 5 7 9 10 8 6 4 2

John Blake Publishing is an imprint of Bonnier Books UK
www.bonnierbooks.co.uk

For all readers,
young and old(er)

Matt Oldfield is an accomplished writer and the editor-in-chief of football review site *Of Pitch & Page*. Tom Oldfield is a freelance sports writer and the author of biographies on Cristiano Ronaldo, Arsène Wenger and Rafael Nadal.

Cover illustration by Dan Leydon.
To learn more about Dan visit danleydon.com
To purchase his artwork visit etsy.com/shop/footynews
Or just follow him on Twitter @danleydon

CONTENTS

ACKNOWLEDGEMENTS

First of all, I'd like to thank John Blake Publishing –
and particularly my editor James Hodgkinson – for
giving me the opportunity to work on these books
and for supporting me throughout. Writing stories for
the next generation of football fans is both an honour
and a pleasure.

I wouldn't be doing this if it wasn't for my brother
Tom. I owe him so much and I'm very grateful for
his belief in me as an author. I feel like Robin setting
out on a solo career after a great partnership with
Batman. I hope I do him (Tom, not Batman) justice
with these new books.

Next up, I want to thank my friends for keeping

me sane during long hours in front of the laptop. Pang, Will, Mills, Doug, John, Charlie – the laughs and the cups of coffee are always appreciated.

I've already thanked my brother but I'm also very grateful to the rest of my family, especially Melissa, Noah and of course Mum and Dad. To my parents, I owe my biggest passions: football and books. They're a real inspiration for everything I do.

Finally, I couldn't have done this without Iona's encouragement and understanding during long, work-filled weekends. Much love to you.

CHAPTER 1

THE BIGGEST FINAL OF ALL

15 July 2018, Luzhniki Stadium, Moscow

One by one, the players walked along the quiet tunnel and out into an amazing spectacle of sound and colour. Yes, it was time for the 2018 World Cup final – France vs Croatia!

The France captain Hugo Lloris led the way, followed by defenders Raphaël Varane and Benjamin Pavard. It was a team full of superstars and their three biggest superstars were at the back of the line:

Kylian Mbappé – the 'next big thing' and the fastest footballer on the planet, Paul Pogba – a powerful midfielder who could play the perfect pass, and last but by no means least, their skilful Number 7, Antoine Griezmann.

Grizou! Grizou! Grizou!

Antoine was already a fans' favourite and a national hero, but if he could help France to win their second World Cup, he would become one of his country's true footballing legends. From Zinedine 'Zizou' Zidane in 1998 to 'Grizou' in 2018.

So far, everything was going according to plan. Antoine had led France all the way to the final, with three key goals and two key assists. When his team needed him most, he hadn't let them down. Whether he was scoring himself or setting up his teammates, Antoine's left foot was lethal!

One more win – that was all France now needed to pick up football's ultimate prize. Antoine was determined to bring joy to his country. He had lost big finals in the past – the 2016 Champions League with Atlético Madrid, Euro 2016 with France – but this was the biggest final of all: the World Cup final.

'And whatever it takes,' he told himself, 'I'm going to win it!'

As the national anthem played, Antoine sang the words loudly and proudly. Although he had left the country at the age of thirteen to move to Real Sociedad in Spain, he still felt French. Mâcon was his home and it always would be. He went back as often as he could to visit his family and friends. They were all cheering him on tonight, whether in the stadium in Russia, or back home on TV.

The France fans were outnumbered by the Croatians but as the match kicked off, they made as much noise as possible.

Allez Les Bleus! Allez Les Bleus!

In the seventeenth minute, Raphaël passed to Antoine, who spun quickly and... *FOUL! – FREE KICK!*

As he got back to his feet, Antoine smiled to himself. It was the perfect position for one of his dangerous deliveries. He had set up Raphaël's goal in the quarter-final and then Samuel Umtiti's goal in the semi-final. Could he keep it up in the World Cup final?

Antoine took a deep breath and waited for the

referee's whistle. Then he curled the ball into the six-yard box and hoped for the best. Could anyone get a touch on it? Raphaël made a late run and leap to reach it but instead, it bounced off Mario Mandžukić's head and into the back of the net. *Own goal – 1–0 to France!*

'Yes, yes, YES!' Antoine roared as he skidded across the grass on his knees, just like he used to do as a kid. It was another key assist to add to his collection. They were on their way to World Cup glory…

But Croatia, like France, were a team who never gave up. Ten minutes later, the score was 1–1. Antoine would have to save the day with another set-piece. From his corner kick, Blaise Matuidi jumped up and missed the ball, but it struck Ivan Perišić on the arm.

'Handball!' the France players argued.

After checking with VAR, the referee said yes. *Penalty!*

Antoine placed the ball down carefully on the spot and took a few steps back. His penalty miss in the 2016 Champions League final was in the past now. France could rely on him; he hadn't missed one in ages.

But should Antoine aim for bottom left or bottom right, top corner, or straight down the middle with a cheeky Panenka chip? No – when the time came, Antoine kept things calm and simple, and sent the goalkeeper the wrong way.

Goooooooooooooooooooooaaaaaaaaaaaaaaaalllllllllllll llllllllllllllll!!!!!!!!!!!!!!!!!!!!

An assist and now a goal – it was turning out to be Antoine's dream final. He celebrated by doing his 'Take the L' *Fortnite* dance, swinging his legs from side to side. His teammates were too cool to join in, but lots of France fans in the crowd did. 'Grizou' was their hero!

In this final in Moscow, the biggest final of all, Antoine was playing with so much confidence. Midway through the second half, he collected a pass from Kylian, did a couple of keepie-uppies in the box and then played it back to Paul. His right-foot shot was blocked, so he tried again with his left. *GOAL – 3–1!*

'Yes, Piochi!' Antoine cheered.

Was that game over? Just in case Croatia were planning an incredible comeback, Kylian made sure with a stunning long-range strike. *4–1!*

'Yes, Kyky!' Antoine screamed.

When the full-time whistle blew, he threw his arms up triumphantly. His Euro 2016 heartache was finally over because now, France were the 2018 World Cup winners!

Even after a tiring tournament, the players still had the energy to run around the pitch hugging each other. What an amazing and emotional moment! What a big team effort! Antoine wiped away his tears with his shirt, but this time, they were tears of pure joy.

'We did it!' he told his best friend, Paul. 'We made the French people proud!'

They could hear the celebrations in the stadium in Russia, and they could picture the scenes back home in Paris. Crowds of fans all around the Eiffel Tower, cheering and waving their flags. And it was all because of them.

The Best Player of the Tournament award went
to Croatia's captain Luka Modrić, but Antoine was
named the Man of the Match in the World Cup final.
It went nicely with his winners' medal and soon, he
would be lifting the greatest prize of all…

Hugo stood in the middle of the French squad,
with the World Cup trophy in his hands. 'Ready?'
he called out. '3, 2, 1…'

'Hurraaaaaaaaay!!!!' everyone roared.

Campeones, Campeones, Olé! Olé! Olé!

It hadn't been an easy journey for Antoine at
all, but thanks to a marvellous mix of talent and
determination, he had made it all the way to the top.
He had achieved his World Cup dream and he had a
simple message for all the clubs that had rejected him
as a boy, for all the ones who had said he was too
small to be a star.

'Look at me now!'

CHAPTER 2

FOOTBALL=MAD IN MÂCON

Zinedine Zidane was from Marseille, Thierry Henry was from Paris, and Youri Djorkaeff was from Lyon. But what about Mâcon? Which of France's famous footballers had grown up there?

Back in the 1990s, the answer was none. Mâcon was a small, quiet, old town on the east side of France, an hour's drive north of Djorkaeff's Lyon. Nothing much happened in Mâcon, least of all sporting success. It had a rugby team and a football team, but neither was particularly good. The local people preferred water sports like rowing, swimming and speedboating.

'Boring!' decided one blond, football-mad boy in

Mâcon. Antoine Griezmann was going to change his town's sporting history forever. From the first moment that he kicked a ball, he fell in love with the beautiful game.

'GOAL!' his dad, Alain, cheered as his three-year-old son ran up and whacked it as hard as he could with his little left foot.

The mini football flew through the air, over the halfway line of the local basketball court, bounced down and then rolled towards the base of the hoop at the other end.

'GOAL!' young Antoine repeated, clapping his tiny hands together. 'Again, again!'

Now that he'd started, there was no stopping him. Antoine was like a puppy with a stick. Each time, he chased after the ball and brought it back to have another go at kicking it.

'Shall we stop for lunch now?' Alain asked after a while. He could hear his stomach rumbling loudly. 'Mummy will be waiting for us and you must be hungry after all that exercise! Don't worry, we can come back and play this afternoon.'

Antoine shook his head stubbornly. 'Again, again!'

'Fine, five more kicks, okay?'

Soon, Alain decided to put up wooden goals to create a proper pitch for his football-mad son. When he saw them, Antoine beamed brightly. Now, he would be able to do less chasing, and more kicking!

'GOAL! GOAL! GOAL!'

As he got older, Antoine did play basketball on that court too, but football was almost always his first-choice sport. At the weekends, he spent hours kicking a ball around with his friends from Les Gautriats, the neighbourhood where the Griezmanns lived. If for some strange reason, they were all busy, Antoine could usually persuade a family member to come out and play goalkeeper.

'Right, that's enough,' his elder sister, Maud, would say after a few shots whizzed past her. 'I'm bored now!'

Antoine shook his head stubbornly. 'Come on, I'm only just getting started!'

'Fine, five more kicks, okay?'

And if for some even stranger reason, none of his

family wanted to play either, Antoine would just
practise his football skills on his own. He became the
King of the Keepie Uppies –

*…forty-seven, forty-eight, forty-nine, FIFTY,
fifty-one…*

– and the Wizard of the One-Touch Pass.

Left foot, right foot, left foot, right foot…

Even on the coldest, wettest winter nights,
Antoine would be out there in front of his house,
in a rain-soaked shirt, kicking the ball against the
garage door again and again.

BANG! THUD!

'Right, that's enough noise for one day,' his mum,
Isabelle, would call out eventually from the doorway.
'If you don't stop now, the neighbours will call the
police!'

Antoine shook his head stubbornly. No, if he
stopped now, he would never become a superstar.
He had to keep practising. 'Please Mum, just a little
bit longer!'

'Fine, five more kicks, okay?'

Antoine just couldn't get enough. His life was

football, football, and more football. It was the only subject that he was interested in.Every morning at George Brassens Primary School, he sat there doodling football cartoons in his exercise books and waiting for the break-time bell to ring. Why? Football!

'Let's play!' Antoine called to his friends as they rushed out of the classroom door.

And every afternoon, he sat there doodling football cartoons in his exercise books and waiting for the home-time bell to ring. Why? Football!

After racing back to drop off his school bag and grab a quick snack, he was ready to go again.

'Let's play!'

Some evenings, he rushed over to the local court for a kickaround with his mates.

And on other evenings, he rushed off to training sessions with his first football club, Entente Charnay-Mâcon 71.

Antoine just couldn't get enough. His life was football, football, and more football. It was the only subject that he was interested in.

CHAPTER 3

MÂCON'S LITTLE MAGICIAN

Entente Charnay-Mâcon 71 was like a second home for Antoine. He was a familiar face at his local football club long before he even started training with the Under-7s. His dad was the coach of the Under-13s, and so he often went along and stood on the sidelines with him.

'My assistant,' Alain liked to call Antoine.

Antoine did like watching football and learning new skills, but playing the game itself was much more exciting. After a few minutes on the sidelines, he usually got bored and wandered off in search of adventure. He soon knew every corner and every cupboard of the club, and the contents of every cupboard too.

'Where did you get that from?' Alain asked when a football magically appeared at his son's feet.

Antoine shrugged. 'I found it behind the goal,' he lied.

His dad just nodded and went back to coaching. He knew that with a football at his feet, his son would be happily occupied for hours.

By the age of five, Antoine was already training with the Mâcon Under-7s. He loved it and never missed a single minute. The activities were really fun and he could feel himself improving: his touch, his passing, his dribbling, his shooting. Everything! However, practice just wasn't the same as playing proper matches.

'When can I make my debut for Mâcon?' Antoine asked his coach for the fiftieth time.

Bruno Chetoux sighed. It didn't seem fair that a boy who wanted to play couldn't play, but the rules were the rules.

'I'm sorry, kid, but you're still not old enough,'

he replied. 'You'll be able to play soon, I promise!'

In the end, Antoine made his debut before
he turned six. There were two reasons for that.
Firstly, Bruno couldn't bear to say no any longer,
and secondly, Antoine was just too talented to be
left out.

In training, he was running rings around everyone.
Once Antoine had the ball, no-one could get it off
him. He could dribble past defenders so easily, like
they were just cones on the ground. There was only
ever one ending – GOAL!

'We need him in our team,' Bruno decided
eventually, '*NOW!*'

'At last!' Antoine cried out when his coach told
him the great news. 'Thanks, I can't wait, it's going
to be amazing!'

He was already imagining all of the goals that
he would score himself, and also all of the goals he
would set up for his teammates.

The strikers were thinking, 'Brilliant, Antoine's
going to create so many chances for us!'

And the defenders were thinking, 'Brilliant, other

teams will have to try and tackle Antoine now, rather than us!'

Fortunately, Antoine lived up to all their expectations. Suddenly, with their new little magician on the left-wing, Mâcon were unstoppable.

Antoine was having the time of his life out there on the football field. It was like having a kickaround on the basketball court with his mates, only a million times better! He had his very own navy-blue football shirt and he had a crowd to entertain with his skills and celebrations.

'Come on, close the blond boy down!' opposition coaches called out as Antoine set off on another mazy dribble. 'Stop him, STOP HIM!'

But as hard as they tried, they couldn't – *GOAL!*

As Antoine slid across the mud on his knees, the spectators talked excitedly about him:

'Wow, that boy's a bit special!'

'What a lovely left-foot!'

Antoine made football look so easy, but as Bruno wondered: was it *too* easy for him? Before long, the coach moved his new star player up to the next age group. Would he be able to shine so brightly against bigger, older boys?

Yes, it turned out. Even at a higher level, Antoine was still Mâcon's little magician. His new team won match after match after match. First, they conquered the local region, and then they travelled further and further to find better teams to beat. Different city, same result. In fact, Antoine got so used to winning that when he didn't, he was absolutely devastated.

'H-how did we l-lose that?' he spluttered tearfully as his dad drove him home.

'These things happen sometimes,' Alain explained. Of course, he wanted to comfort his upset son, but it was also an important lesson for him to learn. 'I know it's not a nice feeling to lose, but we can't win all the time.'

Antoine nodded and wiped away his tears with his shirt. Before long, his champion spirit had returned. Next week, he thought, he would do whatever he could to get his team back to winning ways.

CHAPTER 4

FOOTBALL IN THE FAMILY

'Mum, can Theo come and play football with us today?' Antoine asked one afternoon as he got ready to go out to the court.

Isabelle frowned. 'I don't think so, darling. Not today.'

Her youngest son was still only two years old, and not yet ready for the hustle and bustle of big kid football. It was sweet that Antoine wanted to play with his baby brother, but he would have to find another, older goalkeeper.

'Please!' Antoine begged. 'Don't worry, it'll just be the three of us – me, Maud and Theo. We'll look after him, I promise!'

'Fine, but only for half an hour, okay? And if Theo starts crying, bring him home straight away.'

'Yes, Mum! Thanks, Mum!'

As the three young Griezmanns walked over to the basketball court, Antoine tried to explain the plan to his little brother.

'Today, Theo, we're going to teach you how to play football! What do you think about that?'

His younger brother giggled away.

'He certainly seems excited!' Maud laughed.

As Antoine took up his position in goal, she placed the ball in front of Theo's foot, just like their dad had done for them.

'Ready, steady, KICK!'

Theo swung his leg wildly but somehow the ball bounced and rolled towards the goal. Antoine had a save to make but he knew what he was supposed to do next. He wanted his baby brother to love football too, after all. With a dramatic dive, he let Theo's shot slip straight through his hands.

'Noooooooo!' Antoine groaned, putting on his best acting performance ever.

'GOAL!' cheered Maud.

'GOAL!' young Theo repeated, clapping his tiny hands together. 'Again, again!'

Antoine smiled at his sister. His plan had worked perfectly. 'Great, it looks like we've got another footballer in the family!'

The minutes flew by until Maud checked her watch and panicked. They were going to be late!

'Right, home-time,' she called out. 'Come on, quickly you two!'

After a happy half-hour of dramatic dives and 'GOAL!'s, Theo's first football session was over. They couldn't wait to tell their mum all about it.

'Theo is so good at football already!' Antoine announced eagerly as soon as he walked through the front door. 'He loved scoring lots of goals, didn't he, Maud?'

'Yeah, the only time he cried was when we took the ball away at the end!'

Isabelle laughed. 'Good, I'm glad you had a nice time together. Maybe we'll soon have three more footballers in the family!'

Antoine was confused. Their dad was a football *coach*, but he wasn't a football *player*. 'What do you mean "three *more*", Mum?'

'Well, my dad – your grandad – was a footballer too, remember!'

'Oh yeah, how did I forget that!'

Their grandad, Amaro Lopes, was now pretty old but as a young man growing up in Portugal, he had been a big, strong defender for his local club, FC Paços de Ferreira. His career ended when he moved to France, but he still had photos of his glorious footballing days.

'That's me right there,' he said, proudly showing Antoine one picture. 'Look, I'm almost as tall as our goalkeeper!'

'I hope I grow up to be as tall as you!'

'I'm sure you will!'

Sometimes, the Griezmann family spent their summer holidays back in Paços de Ferreira. Antoine got to visit the FC Paços de Ferreira stadium and watch a match. The team were now playing in the country's top league, against famous clubs like

Porto and Sporting Lisbon.

'Perhaps, you'll play football for Portugal one day!' Amaro said hopefully.

Portugal? Antoine thought for a moment. The 1998 World Cup had changed everything for him. Not only had France won the trophy for the first time ever by beating Ronaldo's Brazil, but Antoine had got the chance to meet all the players before their group game against Denmark.

What a day that had been! Wearing a France shirt with '7' on the back, he ran around excitedly with his best friend Jean-Baptiste, getting all the stars to sign his football: Thierry Henry, Bixente Lizarazu, Fabien Barthez, Robert Pires, Christian Karembeu and, best of all, Zinedine Zidane. Those guys were his new heroes now.

So, when Amaro asked him if he might play for Portugal, he replied firmly. 'Sorry Grandad, I can't. I'm going to play for *Les Bleus!*'

CHAPTER 5

UF MÂCONNAIS

As eight-year-old Antoine prepared to take his next step towards becoming a French superstar, Mâcon made a very important change to their football system. Instead of three different clubs, there would now be just one: Union du Football Mâconnais, or UF Mâconnais for short.

How many youth teams would they have? Would there be enough space for everyone? Many youngsters were worried, but not Antoine. He knew that he was good enough to star for Mâcon's new super-club.

'It's going to be great,' he told Jean-Baptiste. 'Now, we'll get the chance to beat even better teams!'

As part of the big change, UF Mâconnais had moved up to France's fifth division. That was a higher level than he had ever played at before, but Antoine was ready to rise to the challenge. He was still very small and skinny for his age but what he lacked in size, he made up for in spirit. No-one was more desperate to become a professional footballer than the blond boy from Les Gautriats.

'I'm going to make it!' Antoine kept telling himself, and he never stopped believing.

He worked extra hard on the things that he was really good at, like dribbling, passing, and crossing. And he also worked extra hard on the things that he wasn't so good at, like shooting, tackling, and heading. He didn't care that he was the smallest member of the Under-11s; he still wanted to be the best at heading.

At the UF Mâconnais senior team's home games, the junior players sometimes took part in the half-time show. Antoine loved running out onto the pitch with so many faces watching him. It felt like he was a superstar already.

'Jump!' the coaches shouted as they put crosses into the box. The UF Mâconnais youngsters lined up and took it in turns to try and head the ball into the net.

As Antoine leapt high into the air, he watched the cross carefully. It was coming towards him at top speed, but he had to be brave.

'This is it!' he thought to himself. He imagined that it was the last minute of a big cup final and this was his chance to score the winner and become a hero. Antoine used his neck muscles to put extra power on the header, just like his coach had taught him.

Goooooooooooooooooooooaaaaaaaaaaaaaaaalllllllllllll llllllllllllll!!!!!!!!!!!!!!!!!!!!!

For a second, Antoine forgot that he wasn't really playing in a cup final. He turned and threw his arms up in the air triumphantly. Then it hit him: oh yeah, he had made that part up!

'Hey, you do know that you're not Zidane, right?' Jean-Baptiste teased him.

Antoine smiled back. 'Not yet, no, but I will be soon!'

By the time he turned ten, he was already training with the UF Mâconnais Under-13s. Their coach, Christophe Grosjean, had seen Antoine in action many times over the years, but watching him up close at practice, he was more impressed than ever.

In terms of technique, Antoine was untouchable. With the ball at his feet, he could do things that not even Christophe's twelve-year-olds could do. He glided across the grass with the balance, control, and grace of… well, a superstar!

Everyone loved watching Antoine dribble down the wing. It was so exciting. What would he do next? If defenders weren't careful, he quickly made them look like fools. Sometimes, Antoine showed off tricks that he had spent hours learning at home, but a lot of the time, it was just his natural talent shining through.

'When he grows a bit,' Christophe thought to himself, 'he's going to be sensational!'

That was Antoine's only issue; he was still so small and weak for his age. Yes, he had silky skills, but what use was that when big defenders could muscle him off the ball so easily?

'Foul!' he cried out in frustration at first, but his Under-13s coach just shook his head. 'Play on!'

Antoine didn't argue; he just picked himself up and chased after the ball again. Christophe could see that the UF Mâconnais players were being careful with their teammate; real opponents would kick and push him all over the pitch. No, he couldn't let that happen.

'So, when do I get to make my debut?' Antoine asked eagerly one day. He loved the training sessions, but they just weren't the same as playing proper matches.

'Sorry, kid,' Christophe replied as kindly as possible. 'We don't think you're ready just yet.'

Instead, the coach sent Antoine back down to the Under-12s for the rest of the season. Antoine was devastated. It felt like a big step backwards.

'It's so boring here!' he sulked for the first few days but before long, his champion spirit returned. There was only one way to prove Christophe wrong:

Gooooooooooooooooooooaaaaaaaaaaaaaaaalllllllllllll llllllllllllll!!!!!!!!!!!!!!!!!!!!

Gooooooooooooooooooooaaaaaaaaaaaaaaaalllllllllllll llllllllllllll!!!!!!!!!!!!!!!!!!!!

Gooooooooooooooooooooaaaaaaaaaaaaaaaalllllllllllll llllllllllllll!!!!!!!!!!!!!!!!!!!!

A few months later, Antoine was called up to the Under-13s squad again. By then, he was a little taller, a lot tougher, and all set to become a superstar.

'Welcome back!' Christophe said with a smile. He could feel the boy's confidence, burning like a beacon. 'Those defenders don't stand a chance now!'

CHAPTER 6

FOOTBALL DREAMS WITH FRIENDS

The UF Mâconnais youth players were best friends, both on and off the field. Antoine, Jean-Baptiste, Stéphane, Julian and Martin – the boys spent almost all their spare time together. And what was the bond that united them? Football!

On the few weekends when they weren't playing for the Under-13s, they met up to play FIFA on the PlayStation, swap Panini stickers...

Got, got, NEED!

...and, of course, play football. By then, Antoine had mostly left the basketball court near his home behind. He only went there when his brother Theo wanted to practice his shooting. Antoine needed more space for his deadly dribbles and a proper, grass pitch too. Why? So, that he could celebrate his goals by doing awesome knee-slides!

The summer of 2002 was a World Cup summer and they all had their favourite players.

'Today, I'm going to be Thierry Henry!'

'I'll be Zidane!'

'I'll be Ronaldo!

'Oh, I wanted to be him. Fine, I'll be Raúl instead!'

'Okay, who am I?' Jean-Baptiste asked and then started to dance. The others were soon rolling around on the floor laughing.

'Mate, what on earth was THAT?' Stéphane asked. 'Don't ever do that again; it was the worst dance I've ever seen!'

Antoine knew his stuff, though. He guessed the right answer straight away: 'Papa Bouba Diop!'

'See!' Jean-Baptiste beamed happily. 'At least someone's been watching the World Cup!'

Antoine had watched every minute of every match. So, who would he choose to be? He was a huge France fan, but Henry and Zidane were already taken. He was a big fan of the Juventus midfielder, Pavel Nedvěd, but he wasn't playing because the Czech Republic hadn't qualified.

Luckily, Antoine had one last hero he could choose: his greatest hero of all, David Beckham.

'I'll be Becks!' he called out.

Antoine wanted to bend the ball just like Beckham, only with his left foot instead of his right. He spent hours watching videos of his hero's greatest passes, crosses and, best of all, free kicks. There were so many of them:

For Manchester United against Liverpool and West Ham and Barcelona,

And for England against Columbia and Mexico and Greece.

The power, the curl, the accuracy – it was absolutely amazing! 'How does Becks do it?' Antoine marvelled.

And it wasn't just his football skills that Antoine admired. It was his style too – the cool clothes, the classy photos, and the ever-changing haircuts.

Antoine tried his best to copy Becks. His parents

didn't always let him have the latest haircut, but he wore a long-sleeved shirt with the number '7' on the back. That made him feel like Beckham, but could he play like Beckham?

Yes, he could! As he dribbled forward, he looked up and spotted Julian racing down the right wing. It was time to be Becks! In a flash, he pulled back his left leg and played a perfect long-range pass to his teammate. *GOAL!*

'Thanks, Becks!'

'No problem, *Zizou!*'

Their games went on and on, often all day long. If someone had to go home, they could usually find another local kid ready to replace them.

'Right, Robert is on your team now!'

There were only four things that could make their matches end:

1) hunger,

2) heavy rain or snow,

3) darkness, and

4) angry mums and dads.

That particular day, it was darkness that stopped them.

'Okay, next goal wins!' Martin called out as the last of the sunlight disappeared.

'What? That's not fair – our team is winning by four goals!' Jean-Baptiste complained. They were all best friends but once they stepped out onto the football pitch, all that changed – a competitive edge came into play.

'No, you're not!'

'Yes, we are!'

'It's 37–35!'

'No, it's 38–34! That goal didn't count, remember, because Jacques handballed it. And then we scored that one where—'

'Hey, it doesn't matter,' Antoine interrupted. 'Let's just play on and make sure that we score the next goal.'

'Fine,' Jean-Baptiste muttered moodily.

He passed to Antoine who dribbled forward at top speed, past one opponent, then another, then—

'FOUL!' he cried out as he fell to the floor.

'No way, you dived!' Martin argued. 'I won the ball fair and square, and you know it, Becks!'

Antoine wasn't backing down this time. 'As if, Henry! That tackle was worse than that one you did against Uruguay!'

What they really needed was a referee, but eventually, the decision went Antoine's way. *Free kick!*

It was the last minute of the 2002 World Cup Final. This was it – his chance to be the hero. Antoine closed his eyes, took a deep breath, and focused on being Becks.

'Come on, get on with it!' Stéphane shouted. 'We haven't got all night!'

Antoine ran up and struck the ball powerfully, with plenty of curl. It whizzed past the players in the wall and past the goalkeeper too.

Gooooooooooooooooooooaaaaaaaaaaaaaaaalllllllllllll llllllllllllllll!!!!!!!!!!!!!!!!!!!!

Becks had done it; he had won the World Cup! Antoine punched the air and then performed another awesome knee-slide.

CHAPTER 7

TOO SMALL TO BE A STAR?

Antoine got older and a little bit taller, but his life
dream always stayed the same. At school, whenever
he was asked what job he wanted to do in the future,
he wrote down two wonderful words:

'Professional Footballer.'

'It's great to have that ambition,' his teachers
told him, 'but it's a very, very competitive world.
It's best to have other options too. There are lots of
other interesting careers out there. What else do
you like doing?'

Playing football, though, was all Antoine had ever
wanted to do. He knew that it wouldn't be easy, but
he was willing to work and work until he reached his

target. Nothing was going to stop him, and especially not his size.

However, that was more of an issue than ever. Antoine was still a small thirteen-year-old and at that age, French kids switched from playing in smaller nine-a-side spaces to playing on great big eleven-a-side pitches. Suddenly, there was so much space everywhere. It was like taking a tiny goldfish out of its tank and dropping it in the Atlantic Ocean!

Antoine did his best to show off his silky skills as usual, but his little legs couldn't last the whole match. All that running was really exhausting. When the new UF Mâconnais coach, Jean Belver, saw how much he was struggling, he dropped him down to the bench instead.

'Don't worry, you'll get your chance to shine in the second half,' Belver told him.

Antoine *was* worried, though. Being a substitute was unbearable! He couldn't imagine anything worse than sitting there watching as his best friends left him behind. Jean-Baptiste, Stéphane, Martin, Julian

– they were all out there having fun on the football pitch without him.

'I need to get back into the starting line-up!' Antoine told himself through gritted teeth. There was only one way to prove Belver wrong, the next time he got on a pitch:

Goooooooooooooooooooaaaaaaaaaaaaaaaaalllllllllllll llllllllllllll!!!!!!!!!!!!!!!!!!!!

'I'M BACK!' Antoine roared, celebrating with another awesome knee-slide.

At UF Mâconnais, everyone knew Antoine well, and they had full faith in his character. After all, their little blond magician had shown his special champion spirit by bouncing back time and time again. There was no problem whatsoever with his mental strength, and he was working hard to improve his physical strength too.

'Just keep doing what you're doing,' the coach encouraged his left-wing wizard. 'You'll get your growth spurt soon, I'm sure!'

Unfortunately, not everyone shared Belver's belief. During the 2004–05 season, Alain took his son to trials at lots of top clubs all across France. It turned out to be a very tough experience for Antoine.

First, Antoine had a trial for his favourite team, Olympique Lyonnais. It was the closest big club to Mâcon, and he had been a fan ever since his dad took him to his first match at the Stade de Gerland. The adventure, the action, the atmosphere – it was by far the best experience of his life.

'I'm going to play for Lyon when I'm older!' he announced afterwards.

Antoine's favourite player was their Brazilian striker, Sonny Anderson, and amazingly, he got the chance to meet his hero. He was too star-struck to say very much, but he proudly put the photo up on his bedroom wall, next to his posters of Nedvěd, Zidane and Beckham.

So, he was full of excitement when he arrived at the training ground to start his trial. He couldn't wait to become the next Sonny Anderson.

'Hi, Didier! Hi, François!'

Antoine knew most of the Lyon youth coaches already because he attended the club's training camps every summer. They, of course, knew him too – his strengths *and* his weaknesses.

Alain Duthéron was one scout at Lyon who had been keeping a close eye on Antoine for years. Duthéron loved the boy's style, but unfortunately, Antoine's size was still a big problem. At that time, French clubs just weren't looking for small, skilful players; they wanted tall, powerful players. As talented as he was, Antoine didn't fit that description at all.

'I know, but that boy is *special!*' said Duthéron, doing his best to persuade the Lyon youth coaches to be patient with Antoine, but they wouldn't listen. The boy's parents were small too; there was no chance that he would grow up to be big and strong.

'No' – that one short word hurt like a wound, like a punch in the gut. Antoine was devastated, but he picked himself up and carried on.

'There are plenty of other clubs out there,' his dad reassured him, and after one rejection, Antoine wasn't just going to give up. He was determined to achieve his life dream of becoming a professional footballer. No matter what.

Antoine would have to keep reminding himself of that, because there were more hard times ahead.

He was invited to a trial at AS Saint-Étienne, but it was cancelled due to snow.

'We'll try again next time,' his dad said.

He went on trial at FC Sochaux, but like Lyon, they decided that he was too small to be a star.

'We'll try again next time,' his dad said.

He went on trial at AJ Auxerre, but when they took an X-ray of his wrist to predict his future height, the results weren't good. No, they told him, he would always be too small to be a star.

'We'll try again next time,' his dad said.

By then, Antoine really felt like walking away from football, but he didn't. Instead, he went on trial at FC Metz and this time, the club seemed interested in signing him. Finally, was his football dream about to come true? But just when his hopes were up, he heard the same old story:

'Sorry, we think you're too small to be a star.'

Not again! Antoine was too upset to say anything, so his dad spoke up instead.

'You really think my son is too small?' Alain asked angrily. 'Well, we'll see about that!'

How could they say that about Antoine when he was still so young? Kids often didn't get their growth spurt until they were fifteen or sixteen!

'We'll try again next time,' his dad said.

Really? Could Antoine deal with any more disappointments? Fortunately, he wouldn't have to.

CHAPTER 8

SCOUTED BY SOCIEDAD

In Summer 2005, Real Sociedad scout Éric Olhats decided to stop in Paris on his way back from Argentina. He had some football friends in the city who he wanted to catch up with. For Éric, it was just a small change of plan. For Antoine, however, it would turn out to be a life-changing decision.

Montpellier HSC were the latest French club who had offered him a trial. Their scout Manu Christophe was a big fan of Antoine's silky skills, but their youth coach Christophe Blondeau wasn't so sure. The problem? His size, of course.

'Okay, well let's take him to the international

tournament,' they agreed. 'It'll be the perfect way to test how good he really is!'

Alain drove Antoine all the way to Montpellier to meet up with his new teammates. Carrying the club kit in his hands, he boarded the bus heading to Paris.

'Good luck, son!' his dad called out through the car window.

Antoine was excited about playing in such a big tournament, but he wasn't getting his hopes up. After his Metz disappointment, he knew that anything could go wrong. Anything! He might sit on the bench all day, or Montpellier might lose every match and go home early...

'No, I've got to stay positive,' Antoine told himself as he stared out of the bus window. 'I can do this!'

*

That day, Éric's football friends were watching an Under-15s tournament at the Paris Saint-Germain training ground, so he went along to join them. He didn't usually scout youth players for Sociedad but if there was a game going on, he would keep his eyes open for top talent. Éric was a professional, after all.

'Have you spotted anyone special?' he asked his friends.

'Not yet!' they replied hopefully.

The matches were short and played at top speed. The action was end-to-end like a tennis match. Every young player was in a hurry to become the next football hero.

'Slow down and think!' Éric wanted to shout to them, but he didn't.

Eventually, the Real Sociedad scout saw a kid who had the right idea. The little left-winger for Montpellier was a joy to watch. As he dribbled forward, he looked so composed on the ball, like he had all the time in the world.

'That's more like it!'

The more Éric watched, the more interested he became. The blond boy was nowhere near as strong as the other players, but he was easily the best footballer on the pitch. Surely, that was the thing that mattered most?

'When he grows a bit,' the scout thought to himself, 'he's going to be sensational!'

Éric was desperate to know more about the
Montpellier left-winger.

'Is that little blond boy your son?' he asked the
parents on the sidelines, but they all shook their heads.

So, Éric went to speak to the Montpellier coach
instead. After some small talk, he moved on to the
most important topic.

'Your winger has a lovely left foot,' Éric said,
attempting to sound as casual as possible.

'Antoine? Yes, he's a very talented kid,' Blondeau
admitted. 'He's on trial at the moment but sadly
we won't be signing him. He's just not what we're
looking for right now.'

Éric nodded, trying his best to hold back the smile
that was spreading across his face. The scout's mind
was made up; he was going to ask Antoine to come
to Real Sociedad.

But how? And when? He couldn't do anything
without speaking to the boy's parents first, and they
weren't there at the tournament.

Like Antoine, Éric wasn't someone who
gave up easily. He called the Sociedad Sporting

Director, Roberto Olabe, and told him the story of Montpellier's little magician.

'What should I do?' the scout asked.

Olabe's reply was short and simple: 'Just invite the boy to come here for a trial.'

So, during a break between matches, Éric walked over and handed him a folded piece of paper. He had written a message on the top: 'Don't open this until you get home!'

Antoine read it, smiled and nodded. 'Thanks, I won't!'

*

What else was written on that piece of paper? That was the question going around and around Antoine's brain on the long journey back to Montpellier. He held the note tightly in his hand, but he kept his promise to Éric. He didn't look until he was back home with his family.

'Open it! Open it!' Theo chanted impatiently.

'Okay, okay!' Antoine said, unfolding the page at last. As he read it to himself silently, his hands began to shake.

'What does it say?' Maud asked. 'Read it aloud!'

Antoine cleared his throat and then began. 'We would like to invite you to come to Spain for a trial at Real Sociedad.'

'Congratulations! Anything else?'

'There's a name and a phone number at the bottom.'

'Éric Olhats' – soon, the man would feel like part of the Griezmann family. But at first, Antoine's parents were worried.

'I'll call the scout tomorrow,' Alain said cautiously. He just didn't want his son to suffer another disappointment like Metz. 'We'll need to know all the details first.'

'Yes, I'm really not sure about this offer,' Isabelle added. She hated the idea of her son being so far from home. 'Moving to Spain would be a very big step.'

Slowly but surely, however, Éric managed to persuade Antoine's parents to let him go. First, there were long phone calls, and then the scout visited the Griezmann family home. He showed them photos of the Real Sociedad academy and gave them lots of information about schools and training sessions.

'And I'll always be there to look after him,' Éric promised.

Antoine beamed brightly at all the academy pictures. Football in Spain looked awesome, and the best bit was yet to come. Éric had a special gift for him: his first Real Sociedad shirt.

'Cool, thanks!' Antoine said, admiring the shirt's blue and white stripes. He couldn't wait to wear it proudly.

Alain and Isabelle could see how much their son wanted this. How could they say no and dash his dream of becoming a professional footballer?

'Okay, we'll take you to the trial!' they agreed.

Antoine was over the moon. So long, UF Mâconnais – he was setting off on a Spanish adventure!

CHAPTER 9

STAYING STRONG IN SPAIN

Antoine had one trial at Real Sociedad in the spring and then another one in the summer. He really enjoyed both experiences, but had he done enough to impress the youth coach, Iñigo Cortés? Was the club willing to take a chance on a skinny little French kid with a lovely left foot? Yes and yes!

'We'd like to offer Antoine a place at our academy,' Iñigo told the boy's proud parents.

'Thank you, he'll be so happy to hear that!' Alain replied emotionally.

It was the best moment of Antoine's young life, but there would be difficult days ahead. Signing for

Sociedad meant moving to Spain and that meant learning a new language and living a long way from home. That was an awful lot of change for a fourteen-year-old to cope with.

'We're going to miss you!' his mum sobbed as they said their goodbyes at the airport. 'Look after yourself and call us whenever you want to talk!'

At first, Antoine stayed at a boarding school near the border between France and Spain, and then travelled to training every evening. But all that toing and froing soon left him feeling tired, lonely and fed up. One day when Éric went to pick him up, he could see that the boy was very upset.

'What's wrong?' he asked kindly.

Antoine couldn't hold it in any longer. All of a sudden, he burst into tears. 'I want to go home,' he managed to say eventually. He wanted to go back to living with his parents, and Maud and Theo, and to playing football with Jean-Baptiste and Stéphane. 'I hate that school. I don't have any friends there and I miss Mâcon!'

Éric comforted Antoine as best he could. He

wasn't the first young boy to feel homesick at Sociedad. It was only natural.

'Stay strong, kid,' the scout told him. 'Things will get better, I promise!'

Éric had an idea that might help, but he needed to speak to the Sporting Director first. Once Olabe had agreed, Éric asked Antoine, 'Would you like to come and live at my house in Bayonne?'

Bayonne was a French city that was near to the boy's school and also only an hour's drive from San Sebastián, just over the border with Spain and the home of Real Sociedad.

'Yes please!' Antoine agreed eagerly.

Now that they were solving his problems off the pitch, it was time for Antoine to focus *on* the football pitch. With his long blond hair and flashy boots, he arrived at Sociedad looking like a mini mix between Pavel Nedvěd and David Beckham. But did he have the skill to go with the style?

'Just give me the ball and I'll show you!' Antoine said with a cheeky smile. Despite being the new kid in the team, he was full of confidence.

Iñigo liked the confidence and he liked the talent too. He decided to put Antoine in the older age group alongside Sociedad's two other French players, Jonathan Lupinelli and Lucas Puyol. The coach hoped that would help him to feel at home. The plan worked; the trio were soon inseparable, laughing and joking together in their native language.

The only problem with Iñigo's plan was that Antoine was now the youngest player in the team as well as the smallest. He wasn't just going to walk straight into the starting line-up. He still had lots to learn and a lot of improvements to make.

'That's it, Antoine!' his coach encouraged him. 'Keep going!'

Some days, however, it felt too much like UF Mâconnais all over again. Antoine hadn't moved all the way to Spain just to sit on the Sociedad bench!

'You could always come back and play for us again?' Jean-Baptiste often suggested on the phone.

But as tempting as that sounded, Antoine stayed strong. 'No, I'm not giving up now!' he said determinedly.

During each school holiday, Antoine was allowed to return to Mâcon for a few weeks of family, fun and, of course, football with his friends. But when the time came, he always went back to Sociedad, with a brave face and a brand new haircut.

'*Super cool, Grizi!*' Jonathan joked.

For Iñigo and the other Sociedad youth coaches, Antoine was like an awkward piece in a jigsaw puzzle. He was clearly a very special playmaker, with amazing control and creativity, but how could they fit him into the team? In the end, it was the same old answer every time:

'First, he has to grow bigger and stronger.'

Antoine tried to be as patient as possible, but that wasn't easy for a football-mad boy who just wanted to play the game. One year passed, then another, and then another...

Was Antoine making any progress at all? It sometimes felt like his feet were stuck in quicksand. Often when they called, his parents could hear the frustration in his voice.

'You know, you can always come home if you want to,' his mum reminded him.

But as tempting as that sounded, Antoine stayed strong. 'No, I'm not giving up now!' he said determinedly.

Whenever he was feeling low, Antoine talked it through with Éric. That always made him feel better. Éric was always happy to help, whatever the issue. Sometimes, they just sat and chatted about Antoine's life back in Mâcon. And sometimes, they went out onto the football pitch for extra one-on-one training sessions.

Despite all the setbacks, Antoine's passion for his favourite sport never faded. What he lacked in size, he made up for in spirit. He was ready to put in all the hard work necessary to achieve his dream.

'You're going to be great,' Éric reassured him. 'It's only a matter of time before you become a superstar!'

CHAPTER 10

ANTOINE'S BIG BREAKTHROUGH

It was during the 2008–09 season when Antoine really started to shine at Real Sociedad. He was scoring more goals, he was creating more chances, and he was also growing at last. From 5ft 1in, he suddenly shot up to 5ft 9in!

'Where has our lovely little boy gone?' his parents teased him.

And not only was Antoine getting taller, but he was also getting stronger. Finally, he had some extra power out on the pitch and defenders couldn't just push him off the ball. Éric and Iñigo were delighted. That awkward piece of the jigsaw was finally fitting into place!

'There's no stopping him now,' they agreed.

Antoine was still waiting for his big breakthrough moment, though. By the age of eighteen, Becks had been on the verge of making his Manchester United debut. Antoine, on the other hand, still felt far away from the Sociedad first team.

'What can I do to catch Lillo's eye?' he wondered.

Juan Manuel Lillo was the manager of the senior squad, who were struggling down in Spain's Second Division. Scoring goals was their biggest problem, and Antoine could certainly help with that!

Perhaps his big breakthrough would come at Sociedad's famous junior tournament? Becks himself had played there for Manchester United back in the early 1990s. More than fifteen years later, Antoine would get the chance to follow in his hero's footsteps. This time, Sociedad would be competing against Spain's top youth teams, including Barcelona, Valencia and Atlético Madrid.

'Bring it on!' Antoine thought to himself.

All of the Sociedad players were super-excited. The tournament was all they talked about for weeks. Not only would the final take place at the club's main stadium, the Anoeta, but it would also be shown live on Spanish TV.

'Right, we *have* to go all the way and win it!' the youngsters told each other.

First, however, Sociedad had three games in three days against Sevilla, Barcelona, and local rivals Athletic Bilbao. That was an awful lot of football for the Under-19s to play, so their coach, Meho Kodro, had plenty of attacking options to choose from. Would he go with Antoine or Joseba Beitia on the left wing against Sevilla?

When Antoine saw the teamsheet, he punched the air joyfully. 'Thanks, you won't regret this!' he promised his coach.

This was it: Antoine's time to shine. He was going to pay Kodro back with lots of skills and shots...

Goooooooooooooooooooooaaaaaaaaaaaaaaaaallllllllllll llllllllllllll!!!!!!!!!!!!!!!!!!

As the ball rocketed past the Sevilla goalkeeper, Antoine threw his arms up in the air and then slid across the grass on his knees.

'Come on!' he roared.

Antoine was off the mark and suddenly his confidence was sky-high. He scored four more against Bilbao and Barcelona. A new Sociedad star was born, and they were through to the final!

'We always knew you had the talent,' Kodro said with a big smile, 'and now you're really making the most of it!'

Sociedad's opponents at the Anoeta would be Atlético Madrid. With the TV cameras watching, could Antoine add to his five goals and become the hero in the biggest game of all?

Not quite, but he never stopped creating chances for his team. Sociedad took the lead, but Atlético equalised in the last few minutes. Although it was very disappointing, there was no time to despair. The Sociedad players had to lift themselves for the penalty shoot-out!

'Heads up, lads,' Kodro clapped and cheered. 'We can still win this!'

The tension was unbearable. Antoine could hardly watch as, one by one, his teammates stepped up to the spot. He felt sick with the suspense…

GOAL!

'Nice one, Jon!'

GOAL!

'Great strike, Iñigo!'

Eventually, their goalkeeper, Alex Ruiz, dived low to save the day. 4–3 – Real Sociedad were the winners!

'Yesssssssssss!' Antoine screamed as he and his teammates raced over to celebrate with their spot-kick hero. Even winning the World Cup couldn't feel much better than this.

Campeones, Campeones, Olé! Olé! Olé!

Out on the Anoeta pitch, there were hugs and songs, and then medals and trophies. Antoine didn't win the Best Player award, but he did pick up the prize for Top Scorer. What a terrific tournament it had been for him! This was the big breakthrough that he'd been waiting for.

So, what next for Sociedad's new star? Antoine signed a new contract at the club and for the rest of the season, he carried on starring for the Under-19s,

and trying to catch Lillo's eye. Although that
didn't happen, there was soon a new Sociedad
manager to impress. Martín Lasarte's task was to
take the club back up to La Liga, and how was
he going to do that? By giving the youngsters
a chance.

Back home in Uruguay, Lasarte had kick-started
the career of an eighteen-year-old forward called…
Luis Suárez! Could he help Antoine to become the
'next big thing'?

The new Sociedad manager wanted to have at
least two players fighting for every position. It didn't
matter how old they were, as long as they had the
right attitude and the right amount of talent.

Goalkeepers? Tick!

Defenders? Tick!

Central midfielders? Tick!

Right-wingers? Tick!

Strikers? Tick!

There was just one gap that still needed to be
filled.

'What I'm looking for is a tricky left winger,'

Lasarte told the youth coaches. 'Do you have anyone who fits the bill?'

'Yes, we do!' they replied eagerly.

What a stroke of luck! Aged eighteen, Antoine skipped straight past the Reserves and started training with the Sociedad first team.

CHAPTER 11

A SUCCESSFUL START

The first training session with the first-team is a scary moment for any footballer. To some, it feels like being thrown in at the deep end of a pool full of sharks and told to sink or swim.

PANIC!

Not Antoine, though. He had already showed his strong character time and time again to bounce back from rejections and setbacks. He wasn't going to let nerves or youth get in the way of achieving his dream. He was so close now.

'Everyone, this is Antoine,' Lasarte announced to the Sociedad squad. 'He'll be joining us for the next few weeks.'

The older, more experienced players looked across at the young left-winger and grunted. No, they weren't just going to welcome the latest wonderkid with open arms. In fact, quite the opposite; they were going to test his talent and, most importantly, his resilience. Antoine would have to work hard to earn his place in the team.

'Bring it on!' he told himself.

It didn't take long for him to impress Lasarte with his attitude. The Sociedad manager was looking for a determined team player, and Antoine ticked all the right boxes.

For such a skilful player, he wasn't selfish. If a striker was in a better position to score, Antoine always passed.

And for such a skinny player, he wasn't weak. In practice, he battled bravely against the big Sociedad defenders and if he got knocked down, he got straight back up again.

Lasarte liked everything about Antoine. The Sociedad attack needed something a little different, but was the eighteen-year-old ready to be their creative spark? There was only one way to find out – by giving him game-time in the pre-season friendlies.

The manager brought Antoine on for the second half against CD Anaitasuna. From the first time he touched the ball until the final whistle, Antoine dribbled forward with freedom and flair. The poor defenders didn't know what to do to stop him. He twisted and turned his way through and then finished things off with his lethal left foot.

Goooooooooooooooooooooaaaaaaaaaaaaaaaaalllllllllllll llllllllllllllll!!!!!!!!!!!!!!!!!!!!

Goooooooooooooooooooooaaaaaaaaaaaaaaaaalllllllllllll llllllllllllllll!!!!!!!!!!!!!!!!!!!!

What a debut! Antoine was certainly catching the eye, but could he keep it up? Yes, he could! He scored two more in the next match against FC Barakaldo, and then another against SD Eibar.

Just like at the junior tournament, Antoine had taken his chances spectacularly. With five goals in his first four games, he was quickly becoming the talk of the town.

'What do you know about this new wonderkid? "Griezmann" – is he German?'

'No, I'm pretty sure he's French. I really don't know much about him, other than that he's got a lovely left foot!'

Antoine was loving his new life in the Sociedad first team. His manager believed in him and he had passed his teammates' test – he was one of the lads now.

'If you nutmeg me one more time, Grizi, you'll be sorry!' joked the right-back, Carlos Martínez.

'You'll have to catch me first!' Antoine called back cheekily.

He felt ready to be Sociedad's creative spark in the Second Division, but not everyone agreed about that.

'Lots of kids play well in preseason,' some argued, 'but that doesn't mean anything. Remember, he's only eighteen! It's way too soon for him to start in the league.'

When the 2009–10 season kicked off, Antoine had to watch from the sidelines, but he didn't stay there long. Sociedad only won one out of their first four matches, and the fans quickly became frustrated.

'Give Griezmann a go!' they cried out.

Lasarte listened carefully. It was time to see what their young star could do. Antoine came on as a late sub in the Spanish Cup against Rayo Vallecano, and then in the league against Real Murcia, and Gimnàstic, and Girona...

'Come on, Griezmann should be starting!' the Sociedad supporters complained.

Again, Lasarte listened carefully. At home at the Anoeta, he picked Antoine to make his full league debut against SD Huesca.

Antoine couldn't wait to play more minutes. He might not last the full ninety, but he was going to create as many goalscoring chances as possible. He wanted to excite, entertain and, of course, win. His family would all be there to watch him, after all.

'Are you ready for this?' his strike partner, Imanol Agirretxe asked as the two teams lined up in the tunnel.

'You bet I am!' Antoine replied confidently. He could already hear the noise of the crowd, and he

wanted to give them something to cheer even
louder about.

For the first thirty minutes, Antoine struggled to
get into the game. All of Sociedad's attacks were
going down the right wing.

'Over here!' he kept calling for the ball, in acres of
space on the left.

Finally, Antoine got the pass that he wanted.
Right, it was his time to shine, and he had a clever
plan. The Huesca defenders already knew about his
lovely left foot, but did they also know about his
brilliant right?

Not yet! Antoine cut inside and fired off a quick
shot that caught everyone by surprise. The ball
zoomed powerfully past the goalkeeper and into the
bottom corner.

*Goooooooooooooooooooooaaaaaaaaaaaaaaaalllllllllllll
lllllllllllll!!!!!!!!!!!!!!!!!!!*

What a strike! On his first professional start for
Sociedad, Antoine had scored his first goal. He was
off the mark! It was an incredible feeling, one that he
would never, ever forget. He ran towards the corner

flags, swinging his arms wildly. Antoine's cool goal celebrations would come a bit later. Instead, he just stood in front of the fans and kissed the club badge on his shirt.

'I knew you'd score today!' Agirretxe laughed as he gave Antoine a big hug. 'And that'll be the first of many, mate. Congratulations!'

CHAPTER 12

SOCIEDAD'S YOUNG STAR

What next for Sociedad's new Number 27? Well, Antoine kept starring – and his team kept winning! The doubters had disappeared; he was a fans' favourite already.

Against Salamanca, in October 2009, Xabi Prieto tapped a quick free kick to Dani Estrada, who crossed the ball into the six-yard box. Antoine made a striker's run ahead of Agirretxe and got there just in time. 1–0!

Goooooooooooooooooooooaaaaaaaaaaaaaaaallllllllllll llllllllllll!!!!!!!!!!!!!!!!!!

'Come on!' Antoine yelled out as his happy teammates hugged him.

Despite being the new kid, he had already set himself a new challenge: leading Sociedad back into La Liga, the top division of Spanish football. Next season, Antoine wanted to be playing against Barcelona and Real Madrid, and their superstars Lionel Messi and Cristiano Ronaldo.

Only the top three teams in the Second Division would win promotion, however, and after two surprise defeats, Sociedad started to slip down the table. Would they have to wait another year?

'No way!' Antoine declared. He wasn't giving up yet, not until the very last kick of the season.

Against Recreativo de Huelva, Antoine raced down the left wing and skipped past a sliding tackle. As he dribbled into the penalty area, he looked up and crossed towards Agirretxe. But just as the striker looked certain to score, the goalkeeper stretched out an arm and pushed the ball away.

'Ohhhhhhhhhhhhhhhhhhhhh!' groaned the Sociedad players and supporters in the Anoeta stadium.

Then just before half-time, Antoine curled a

brilliant free kick into the box, but Ion Ansotegi's header bounced back off the post.

'Ohhhhhhhhhhhhhhhhhhhhh!' they all groaned again.

With twenty minutes to go, Sociedad still hadn't scored. A draw wouldn't do; they had to win!

The rain was lashing down, but Antoine battled on. All he needed was one good goalscoring chance…

ZOOM! He raced past the Recreativo right-back and collected a pass on the edge of the area. This was it; he just had to stay calm. Antoine waited until the defenders were closing in, before shooting straight through the goalkeeper's legs. *Nutmeg!*

Gooooooooooooooooooooaaaaaaaaaaaaaaalllllllllllll llllllllllllll!!!!!!!!!!!!!!!!!!

Eighteen-year-old Antoine had saved the day for Sociedad; he was the hero! Now, how should he celebrate his big moment? He jumped over the advertising boards, and then spotted an empty chair.

'A-ha – perfect!' Antoine thought to himself. He sat down in the chair and started clapping like he was a supporter in the crowd!

'You're crazy, kid,' his teammate Carlos Bueno
called out, 'and we love you for that!'

Sociedad stayed in the Top Three for the rest
of the season, with Antoine playing almost every
minute of every match. Not only that, but he was
also taking free kicks and corners like his hero,
Becks. It was an amazing experience for such a
young footballer. He had the support of his manager,
his coaches, his teammates, *and* the fans. They
were his second family and they gave him the
confidence to show off his silky skills.

When a cross came in from the right wing,
Antoine didn't bother taking a touch to control the
ball; instead, he hit it first time with his right foot on
the volley.

*Goooooooooooooooooooaaaaaaaaaaaaaaaalllllllllllll
lllllllllllllll!!!!!!!!!!!!!!!!!!!*

Wow, what a superstrike! As he ran towards the
corner flag, Antoine leapt high into the air.

His reputation was on the rise too. Word quickly
spread about Sociedad's young star. Scouts came from
all over Europe to see Antoine in action, and they

liked what they saw. There was interest from Lyon, Arsenal, and even Becks's old club, Manchester United! Yes, Antoine was a wanted man, and Sociedad would have to act fast if they wanted to keep him.

They did. Soon, he was signing a big new five-year contract at the club. If one of the top teams really wanted to buy him, they would have to pay £30 million.

'Right, let's win the league now!' Antoine cheered happily.

With four games to go, Sociedad were top of the table with Levante, but only on goal difference. To claim the title, they had to keep winning and hope that Levante lost.

Sociedad beat Villarreal B, and Levante beat Rayo Vallecano. The two teams were tied on sixty-eight points!

'Hey, there's no need to panic,' Lasarte warned his players. 'Just play your normal way and we'll get those three points!'

Antoine was fully focused on achieving his target:

playing in La Liga. Away at Cadiz, he curled in another fantastic free kick and Carlos headed home. *GOAL!* Sociedad won 3–1 and their weekend got even better when Levante lost. They were now three points clear at the top. If they could just beat Celta Vigo, the Second Division title would be theirs!

The Anoeta Stadium was absolutely packed for the biggest game of the year. Everywhere that Antoine looked, he saw the colours of Sociedad.

Blue-and-white striped shirts,

blue-and-white striped scarves,

blue-and-white striped banners,

and even blue-and-white striped faces!

The supporters were nervous, but they still sang the club songs loudly and proudly.

'*Vamos, Real!*' they cheered.

What an atmosphere! If Sociedad won, it would be party time in the streets of San Sebastián. They couldn't let their fans down now...

Celta started well but Sociedad grew stronger as the game went on. Early in the second half, Carlos flicked the ball to Antoine, and he dribbled forward at top speed.

'Go on! Go on!' the fans urged him on.

This was it; his chance to win the title for his team. But as Antoine entered the penalty area, a defender came across and tripped him.

'Penalty!' he cried out as he lay there, sprawled across the grass.

When the referee pointed to the spot, the stadium went wild.

'We're going to win the league!' the fans shouted excitedly.

Xabi stepped up and… *GOAL – 1–0!*

Sociedad were so close now. Could they hold on to their lead?

Ten minutes later, Antoine battled bravely for a header at the back post. Too small to be a star? No way! He jumped the highest and headed it down for Carlos to score. *2–0!*

What a way for Antoine to end his incredible debut season! Six goals, lots of amazing assists, and now the Spanish Second Division title. It was beyond his wildest childhood dreams.

As soon as the final whistle went, the Sociedad players got the party started. Antoine, of course, was at the centre of all the fun. One minute, he was diving across the grass again and the next, he was dancing on Franck Songo'o's shoulders. He felt like Superman. It was easily the best night of his life so far.

Campeones, Campeones, Olé! Olé! Olé!

Unfortunately, Antoine didn't have very long to enjoy the moment. There would be no summer holiday for him that year, no well-deserved break. Instead, a few weeks after winning the league in Spain, he was heading home to France for the Under-19 European Championship.

CHAPTER 13

FRANCE'S YOUNG STAR

Yes, after his successful season in Spain, Antoine had attracted France's attention. It turned out that his country hadn't forgotten him, after all.

'Wow, thanks!' he told the Under-19s coach, Francis Smerecki, when he got the great news about his first international call-up.

Although Antoine didn't live in France any more, his family did, and he still felt French. Mâcon was his home and it always would be, no matter where he played his club football. Therefore, it was a huge honour for him to represent his country.

Antoine couldn't wait to wear the famous blue shirt. In only his second match for the Under-19s, he scored the winning goal against Ukraine. Smerecki had seen enough; he named Antoine in his squad for the UEFA 2010 Under-19 European Championship.

'I don't mind giving up my summer holiday for that!' Antoine joked with his brother, Theo.

Along with Spain, France were the favourites to win the whole tournament. They had home advantage and an excellent squad too. Their attack included Chelsea's wonderkid Gaël Kakuta, Lyon's Alexandre Lacazette, and now Antoine as well.

When the France senior team were knocked out in the first round of the 2010 World Cup, there was even more pressure on the Under-19s to perform well.

'Come on, let's lift that trophy!' Smerecki urged his players. France had lost in the semi-finals in both 2007 and 2009. This time, they were good enough to go all the way.

But what part would Antoine get to play? He was the new kid in the squad, and the others nicknamed him 'The Spaniard'. It wasn't a nasty nickname, but it did make him feel like the odd one out. Most of his teammates played for French clubs, and they had been playing together for years. Lots of them had been part of the France Under-17s team that lost to Spain in the Euro final two years earlier.

Oh well – Antoine would just have to work and work until he forced his way into the team. He was good at that!

France got off to a very strong start. In their first match, they thrashed the Netherlands 4–1. Antoine didn't manage to score, but he did in the second match against Austria. He grabbed two goals and so did Alexandre, in a 5–0 win.

'We're just too hot to handle!' they joked as they celebrated together.

Antoine was having the time of his life. The small, skinny boy from Mâcon was well on his way to becoming a superstar.

'"Griezmann" – remember the name!' his dad told people proudly.

France were on fire – could anyone stop them? Croatia did their best to beat them. They took the lead in the semi-final, but it didn't last long. Gaël got the equaliser and then Cédric Bakambu scored a late winner.

'Yes, you legend – we're in the final!' Antoine cheered as he chased after France's hero.

Their opponents in the final would be Spain, Antoine's second country. He had seen lots of their players in action and he knew how dangerous they could be. Thiago Alcântara was a midfield magician and Rodrigo could score from any angle. It was definitely going to be France's toughest test yet.

'We've got nothing to fear tonight,' Smerecki told the players before the big kick-off in Caen. 'Just go out there and make your country proud!'

Antoine was determined to become a national hero. As soon as the match started, he buzzed around the pitch, calling for the ball.

'Over here – pass it!'

Unfortunately, Antoine hardly had a touch because Spain were on top. They scored first and they nearly got a second.

'Keep going, we'll turn things around!' Antoine tried to encourage his teammates.

But France needed to get a goal quickly before it was too late. They had the home crowd behind them, but they were losing the battle out on the pitch.

'What's wrong?' Smerecki asked Antoine at half-time. He could see that his left winger was wincing with pain.

'It's nothing. My ankle hurts a bit, but I'll be fine to carry on!'

Antoine desperately wanted to keep playing, but instead, his manager decided to make a bold substitution. On came Yannis Tafer, and off went Antoine.

It was disappointing news, but Antoine didn't storm off in a sulk. No, he was too much of a team player to do that. If he couldn't help France out on the field, then he would try to help them from the bench instead.

'Come on, we can still win this!'

'Allez Les Bleus!'

When Yannis set up Gilles Sunu to make it 1–1, Antoine jumped up out of his seat just like all the other France supporters. He punched the air passionately. France were back in the game!

It was a fascinating final between two very talented teams, but there could only be one winner...

FRANCE! When his friend Alexandre headed in the winning goal, Antoine hobbled down the touchline to join in the big squad hug.

'Congratulations, I knew we could do it!' he shouted gleefully.

The France Under-19s were the Champions of Europe! Winning was a team effort and each of the players had played their part in the glorious success. Antoine hadn't been their hero in the final, but he had played well enough to make the Team of the Tournament, alongside Gaël and Cédric.

With a winners' medal around his neck and the glistening trophy in his hands, Antoine felt on top of the world. Could his life get any better? It could! The Under-19 Euros was only the start of Antoine's international adventures with France.

CHAPTER 14

LIGHTING UP LA LIGA

When he returned to Spain after his Euro success, Antoine had some catching up to do. Real Sociedad told him to take two weeks off, but after only a few days, he was desperate to get back out on the football pitch.

'Can I come back early?' Antoine asked Lasarte. 'Please, I'm so bored!'

Plus, he didn't want to miss any more of the pre-season training. What if someone else had caught the manager's eye while he was away? Sociedad were playing in La Liga now, against top teams like Barcelona and Real Madrid. So, maybe Lasarte would choose a more experienced winger...

'I'm back!' Antoine wanted to shout from the rooftops. 'Remember me?'

There were several new faces at the club. Sociedad had signed two new strikers, two new attacking midfielders... and a new left-winger. *Uh-oh!* Antoine would be competing with Francisco Sutil for one starting spot.

'Don't worry – if you play like you did last season,' Lasarte reassured him, 'you'll keep your place, no problem!'

Competition was good; it always brought out the best in Antoine. With his manager's support and his favourite Number 7 shirt, he was ready to spring into action. He would make his full La Liga debut against... Real Madrid!

'No big deal,' Antoine tried to tell himself, but it *was* a big deal. This was the moment he'd been dreaming about ever since he first joined Sociedad as a skinny little boy. This was the opportunity that he'd been waiting for, to test himself against Ronaldo and co.

In the first half, Sociedad's two big chances both

fell to Antoine. First, he snuck past the daydreaming Sergio Ramos to reach Xabi's cross.

'Here we go!' the Sociedad fans cheered, rising to their feet in excitement.

It was a free header in front of goal, and if he scored it, Antoine would be a club hero forever. Unfortunately, he didn't. He put way too much power on the header and the ball flew high over the crossbar.

'No! What a waste!' he screamed, swatting the air angrily.

A few minutes later, Raúl Tamudo played a great through-ball and Antoine sprinted past Ramos again.

'Here we go!' The Sociedad fans were back up on their feet. This time, they were even more excited because the ball was at Antoine's feet, rather than on his head. What could go wrong?

Antoine took one touch to control it and then *BANG!* But instead of trusting his right foot, he struck it awkwardly with the outside of his left foot. The shot whizzed just wide of the post.

'Not again!' he screamed in disbelief. He stood

there frozen with his hands on his head, and so did his teammates.

Oh dear, would his manager be angry with him? No – at half-time, Lasarte was full of encouragement. 'Keep going, you're causing them all kinds of problems!' he told Antoine.

It was Real Madrid who scored first, but Sociedad equalised straight away, and that was all thanks to Antoine, their danger man. He set up Raúl with a fantastic, fizzing free kick. *1–1!*

'Come on!' Antoine roared with a mix of joy and relief.

In the end, Ronaldo won the game with a free kick of his own, but Antoine didn't let that get him down. He was holding his own at the highest level. He was competing with the best players in the world now.

Antoine had his first La Liga assist, but what about his first La Liga goal? As each game passed, he grew more and more desperate to score, but that didn't help at all. He was hurrying shots and trying too hard.

'Just don't think about it,' Raúl replied when Antoine asked him for advice. 'You're playing well and that's what matters!'

When Antoine did finally get his first La Liga goal against Deportivo de La Coruña, it wasn't a very special strike. His celebration, however, was very special indeed. He jumped over the advertising boards at the Anoeta, and then spotted an empty car parked behind the goal.

'A-ha – perfect!' he thought to himself.

'Follow me!' he called to his teammates.

Antoine climbed into the front seat and started turning the steering wheel like he was driving the car! His teammates soon filled up the passenger seats.

'Grizi, you're crazy,' Xabi called out, 'and we love you for that!'

Now, that he was off the mark, Antoine could carry on lighting up La Liga. His manager kept his promise, and Antoine kept his place in the Sociedad team. Francisco who? Lasarte knew who his best left winger was.

Antoine scored in important victories over Málaga

and Getafe, and he set up goals against Sevilla and Atlético Madrid. What a superstar!

He knew that his main job was keeping Sociedad safe, but he liked to entertain as well whenever he could. For him, football was about winning *and* having fun. When he scored his second goal against Sporting Gijón, he celebrated by standing with one of the stadium stewards.

'I love this club!' Antoine said, looking up at all the singing, dancing fans.

At the age of nineteen, he was learning how to be the best by playing against the best. La Liga was the greatest football education ever!

Messi's Barcelona battered Sociedad 5–0 at the Nou Camp, but it was a different story at home at the Anoeta. Antoine and his teammates fought back from 1–0 down to beat the league leaders 2–1.

'We did it!' the players cried happily as they hugged each other. 'We're staying up!'

It was a historic win that saved Sociedad from being relegated back to the Second Division.

In the second match of the 2011–12 season,

however, the stars of Barcelona returned to the
Anoeta, eager for revenge.

Alexis Sánchez passed to Xavi. *1–0!*

Xavi passed to Cesc Fàbregas. *2–0!*

Was it game over already, after only twelve
minutes? The Sociedad supporters feared the worst,
but down on the pitch, their players persevered.

Xabi crossed to Agirretxe. *2–1!*

'Yes, we can do this!' Antoine shouted, throwing
his arms up in the air.

Agirretxe's next shot hit the crossbar but Antoine
raced in to score the rebound. 2–2!

*Goooooooooooooooooooooaaaaaaaaaaaaaaaalllllllllllll
llllllllllllll!!!!!!!!!!!!!!!!!!!*

What a comeback! Even when Messi came on,
Sociedad stayed strong.

At the final whistle, Antoine punched the air with
passion. This was where he belonged now – at La
Liga's highest level, battling it out with Messi and
Ronaldo.

CHAPTER 15

INTERNATIONAL UPS AND DOWNS

France's Under-19 Euro winners were soon off on another big international adventure: to the FIFA Under-20 World Cup in Colombia.

Yippeeeeeee!

Antoine was full of excitement as the squad set off for South America. He couldn't wait to get started. The Under-20 World Cup was a very special tournament with so much history. Diego Maradona had been the star player back in 1979, then Messi in 2005, and Sergio Agüero in 2007. Could it be Antoine's turn in 2011? Hopefully! He was ready to shine with the eyes of the world watching him.

France's first match was against Colombia,

the hosts. Their coach warned them about the atmosphere before kick-off.

'It's going to be really loud out there tonight,' Smerecki said. 'So, try your best to ignore the boos and get on with the game, okay?'

'Yes, Coach!'

When Gilles scored, France looked like they would cruise to a comfortable victory. But instead, they were destroyed by Colombia's deadly duo, James Rodríguez and Luis Muriel. Out on the left-wing, Antoine couldn't believe what he was seeing. The goals just kept going in.

1–1, 2–1, 3–1, 4–1 to Colombia!

It was a really embarrassing result for France, but their World Cup wasn't over yet. If they won their next two matches, they would still go through.

France 3–1 South Korea,

France 2–0 Mali.

Job done! They were in the second round, but that didn't satisfy Antoine. So far, he didn't have a single goal or assist in the tournament. He was playing his worst football in ages.

'You guys play better when I'm not on the pitch,' he argued grumpily.

'Rubbish!' Gaël replied. 'We need you, Grizi. You'll get a goal soon!'

Antoine nearly scored in the first half against Ecuador. His free kick curled high over the wall and only just wide of the post.

'Nearly!' he groaned.

The minutes ticked by and still France couldn't score a winning goal. Antoine set up glorious chances for Clément Grenier and Cédric but they both missed the target.

It was no good; Antoine would have to score the winner himself, and he didn't have long left to do it. In fact, if he didn't do something special soon, Smerecki would take him off. Gaël and Alexandre were on the bench, watching and waiting.

'It's now or never,' Antoine muttered to himself.

As he chased after another hopeful long ball, the Ecuador defenders called, 'OFFSIDE!' but the linesperson's flag stayed down.

Antoine was through on goal, one on one with the

keeper to win the match for France! His first shot was saved but not his second.

Goooooooooooooooooooooaaaaaaaaaaaaaaaaalllllllllllll llllllllllllll!!!!!!!!!!!!!!!!!!!!

Antoine had done it; at last, he was a World Cup hero! He ran over to celebrate with the substitutes behind the goal. Winning was a team effort, after all.

At the final whistle, the France players hugged and high-fived. Thanks to Antoine, they were through to the quarter-finals. And after 120 tense minutes of football against Nigeria, they were through to the semi-finals! Portugal were now the last team standing between France and the Under-20 World Cup Final.

'Come on, we're so close!' Smerecki urged his players on.

But unfortunately, France conceded two goals in the first half and this time, they couldn't fight back. Despite Antoine's best efforts, his World Cup dream was over... for now.

'Never mind, in a few years, we'll be playing in the senior tournament,' Alexandre declared confidently as they clapped the French fans in the stadium. 'World Cup 2014 – see you there, bro!'

Antoine nodded and managed a small smile. It was disappointing, but he did feel like he was on the path to international glory. From the Under-20s, he soon moved up to the Under-21s and from there, it would only be one short step to the senior squad.

'It's only a matter of time,' his proud brother, Theo, assured him.

That last short step, however, turned out to be a giant leap. It would be nearly three long years before Antoine made his senior debut for France.

It was all because of one silly mistake. In October 2012, the France Under-21s faced Norway in the play-offs to qualify for Euro 2013. When they won the home leg 1–0, the young players were in the mood to celebrate.

'Hey, we're only halfway there,' their manager, Erick Mombaerts, warned them. 'We've still got to win the second leg in Norway next week.'

Unfortunately, some members of the squad didn't listen. Five young players decided to sneak out of the team hotel to go partying, and Antoine was one of them. When Mombaerts found out the next day, he was furious.

'You're meant to be professional footballers!' the Under-21 manager shouted. 'We've got a game in three days and we need to prepare, not party. You've really let yourselves and your country down.'

That second leg turned out to be a total disaster for France. With twenty minutes to go, Norway were winning 5–1! Antoine came on and scored, but it was too little too late. France wouldn't be playing at Euro 2013 after all.

Antoine felt very embarrassed and ashamed of himself. He had made a silly mistake, and he had paid the price for it. It was an important lesson for a young player to learn.

'I'm sorry, it won't happen again!' he promised Mombaerts.

A month later, however, Antoine was banned from the French national teams for a whole year. During that time, he couldn't play for the Under-21s *or* the seniors.

'No way, that's not fair!' Antoine protested at first, but it was no use. He had to accept his punishment and just wait for it to end.

'You know you could always play for Portugal instead…' Theo suggested one day during that difficult year.

Yes, thanks to their Grandad Amaro, that was still a possibility for Antoine. He did think about it briefly, but not for very long. He was born in France and he felt 100 per cent French. Plus, he was determined to follow in the footsteps of his idols, the heroes of 1998: Barthez, Lizarazu, Henry and, best of all, Zidane.

Yes, Antoine would just have to wait for his turn to be a French hero.

CHAPTER 16

SOCIEDAD'S SHINING STAR

While he waited to make his international
comeback, Antoine carried on shining for his club,
Real Sociedad. The fans loved their little French
magician, or 'The Little Devil' as they now called
him. Each season, Antoine got better and better.
After scoring seven goals in his first year, he then
scored eight in the next, and then eleven in the
year after that.

During the 2012–13 season, Antoine helped take
Sociedad from mid-table all the way up into the La
Liga Top Six. No, they weren't on the same level as
Barcelona and Real Madrid yet, but they did have a
fantastic front four: Agirretxe up front, with Xabi just

behind, then Carlos Vela on the right and, of course, Antoine on the left.

'There's no stopping us now!'

Not only was he getting more goals, but Antoine was also getting more important goals. He scored in both of Sociedad's local derby wins against Athletic Bilbao, and in a thrilling draw with Real Madrid. This time, when the cross came to him at the back post, Antoine didn't waste his chance.

Goooooooooooooooooooooaaaaaaaaaaaaaaaaalllllllllllll llllllllllllll!!!!!!!!!!!!!!!!!!!

'Come on!' Antoine roared as he leapt up, swinging his fist at the sky.

With one game to go, Sociedad were in fifth place, two points behind Valencia. If they finished fifth, they would qualify for the Europa League. But if they finished fourth, they would qualify for the greatest club competition on earth, the Champions League.

'We *have* to win this!' Antoine told his teammates before their final match against Deportivo de La Coruña.

Playing in the Champions League had been

Antoine's childhood dream. As a young boy in Mâcon, he had watched Nedvěd, Zidane and Beckham all starring on football's biggest stage. Was he about to get his chance at last? Sociedad were so close, and Valencia had a tough trip to Sevilla. Anything could happen...

But first things first: Sociedad had to win at Deportivo.

Carlos dribbled through the defence and took a shot, but the keeper made a comfortable save.

'Unlucky!' Antoine clapped to encourage his teammate.

After twenty minutes, Sociedad's star wingers swapped places. On the left, Carlos collected the ball and passed it through to Agirretxe.

'Over here!' Antoine called out, waving his arms in the air. He was in so much space on the right.

Agirretxe decided to strike it himself, but the rebound fell right at Antoine's feet. This was it – his chance to be the hero who shot Sociedad into the Champions League! As the goalkeeper rushed across his line, Antoine coolly aimed for the opposite corner.

The ball clipped the post on its way into the net.

Goooooooooooooooooooaaaaaaaaaaaaaaaaalllllllllllll llllllllllllllll!!!!!!!!!!!!!!!!!!!!!!

There was no cool celebration – not yet. Antoine was saving that for when they won the match and qualified for the Champions League. At half-time, it was all looking good. Sociedad were 1–0 up and Valencia were 2–1 down.

'Just stay focused on our own match!' Sociedad's manager Philippe Montanier urged.

Sociedad didn't score a second goal, but they held on to their lead. Valencia, meanwhile, had lost 4–3 to Sevilla...

As the referee blew the final whistle, Antoine booted the ball high into the stands. 'We did it!' he cheered, throwing his arms up triumphantly.

Agirretxe was the first to run over and give him a big hug. 'You're a club legend now!' he cried out.

Thanks to Antoine's goal, Sociedad had finished in fourth place in La Liga. Next season, they would be playing in the Champions League!

They wouldn't go straight into the group stage,

however. First, they would have to win a play-off against...

...Lyon! The team that Antoine had supported as a boy, and the team that had decided that he was too small to be a star! He couldn't wait to show them what a mistake they had made.

For the first leg, Antoine travelled back home to France and back to the Stade de Gerland where his dad had taken him to see his first ever football match.

'Good luck!' he said to his friend from the France Under-20s, Alexandre. They would be playing on opposite teams.

'Yeah, may the best team win!' replied Alexandre.

Antoine was going to make sure that was Real Sociedad. He had even dyed his hair bright blond for the big occasion.

Early in the first half, Carlos chased down the left wing and looked up for the cross. Was there anyone there? Yes, Antoine was racing into the penalty area...

The ball was behind him, but in a flash, Antoine

swivelled his body and went for the spectacular. He jumped up and swung his left foot forward. *BANG!* His technique was perfect and so was his power and direction. The ball flew into the bottom corner before the goalkeeper had even moved.

Goooooooooooooooooooooaaaaaaaaaaaaaaaaaallllllllllll llllllllllllllll!!!!!!!!!!!!!!!!!!!!

On his return to Lyon, Antoine had just scored his best goal ever! With the adrenaline rushing through him, he felt like a superstar – no, a super*hero*. He ran over and jumped into Carlos's arms.

'Yes, yes, YES!'

In the second half, Haris Seferović scored another wondergoal for Sociedad.

'That was almost as good as mine!' Antoine joked as they celebrated together.

It finished 2–0 in France, and eight days later, it finished 2–0 in Spain. At home at the Anoeta, Antoine didn't score but he did set one up for Carlos. Sociedad were through to the Champions League group stage!

Their opponents would be Shakhtar Donetsk,

Bayer Leverkusen, and Becks's old club, Manchester United.

'Bring it on!' Antoine said with a cheeky smile. 'The Little Devil' was ready to give Europe's top defenders a trip to hell and back.

Unfortunately, it didn't work out that way. No, Antoine didn't enjoy his first Champions League experience at all. Sociedad lost five of their six games, and they only scored one goal – a penalty taken by Carlos.

Against Manchester United, Antoine hit a fierce, curling free kick but it struck the post. *So close!*

'Oh well, there's always next time,' he told himself as he trudged off the Old Trafford pitch after a 1–0 defeat.

There was no way that he was going to let that be his one and only Champions League adventure.

CHAPTER 17

WORLD CUP 2014

At the start of 2014, the ban on Antoine playing for
France was finally lifted. Hurray – his silly mistake
was behind him at last! He now had six months to
force his way into the senior squad before the start of
the 2014 World Cup in Brazil.

'Easy!' he declared confidently.

The problem was that France's first international
match of the year wasn't until March. Oh well, he
would just have to keep shining for Real Sociedad
and hope that the national manager was watching.

Fortunately, Didier Deschamps was watching
Antoine closely:

He saw his thundering strike against Athletic

Bilbao, his cheeky lob and powerful header against Elche, and his marvellous performance against Messi's Barcelona too.

With the score at 1–1, Carlos crossed to Antoine, who slid in to chip the ball over Víctor Valdés.

Goooooooooooooooooooaaaaaaaaaaaaaaaaalllllllllllll llllllllllllll!!!!!!!!!!!!!!!!!!!

Five minutes later, Antoine set up Sociedad's third goal with a clever pass to David Zurutuza.

Deschamps was very impressed. Antoine could play in all three attacking positions – right wing, left wing, or even striker! That made him a very useful addition indeed. When the manager picked his squad for France's match against the Netherlands, there was a new name next to Franck Ribéry, Olivier Giroud and Karim Benzema:

'A. Griezmann.'

'I'm in!' Antoine told his family straight away.

'Congratulations, we're so proud of you!' his parents cried.

'What did I tell you?' Theo laughed. 'It was only a matter of time!'

Antoine didn't merely make his international debut as a substitute; he played right from the start. With Franck out injured, the France front three was Karim in the middle, Mathieu Valbuena on the right, and Antoine on the left. What a moment! His whole family was there at the Stade de France for his big day.

'We love you, Antoine!' they cheered proudly.

Antoine felt emotional just walking out onto the pitch wearing his country's famous blue shirt. By the time the national anthem began, he was almost in tears.

'Not now,' he told himself, 'this is my time to shine!'

Mathieu crossed the ball to Antoine, who passed it first-time to Karim on the volley. His header was going in, but it was blocked on the goal line.

'Excellent!' Deschamps clapped on the sidelines.

France went on to beat the Netherlands 2–0. Antoine didn't get a debut goal or assist, but he was off to a strong start.

What next? Antoine was hungry for more international action, but he would have to wait another two months. By then, Deschamps had already named his squad for World Cup 2014 and… Antoine was in!

'Yes!' he cheered with his fists clenched. 'Brazil, here I come!'

Before that, however, France had three friendlies to play. If he wanted to be a World Cup hero, Antoine would need to do something special…

It didn't happen against Norway, but it did happen against Paraguay. With ten minutes to go, the ball came to Antoine on the edge of a crowded penalty area.

'Now's your chance!' he told himself. 'Don't waste it!'

Time seemed to stand still as Antoine controlled the pass and then curled a looping shot over every head and down into the bottom corner.

Goooooooooooooooooooooaaaaaaaaaaaaaaaaalllllllllllll llllllllllllllll!!!!!!!!!!!!!!!!!!!!

It was definitely special! Antoine chose his favourite celebration for his first international goal – an awesome knee-slide.

'*Allez Les Bleus!*' he roared like a lion.

In the final friendly against Jamaica, Antoine only came on with twenty minutes to go, but he still managed to score two goals. The second was even a cheeky backheel! But had he done enough to earn a World Cup starting spot? He would have to wait and see.

Antoine had played at the 2011 Under-20 World Cup in Colombia, but that was nothing compared to this. This was an international celebration of football in the best possible place – Brazil! Everywhere the players went, there was a real party atmosphere – the beaches, the stadiums *and* the streets.

'Right, time to focus on football!' Antoine told himself.

For France's first game against Honduras, Franck was out, and that meant Antoine was in. Wow, his World Cup dream was really coming true.

In the first-half, France hit the crossbar twice: first, Blaise Matuidi, and then Antoine with a header.

'Noooooo!' he groaned with his hands on his head. What a missed opportunity to score on his

World Cup debut! Instead, it was Karim who became France's hero.

In France's second group match, against Switzerland, Antoine was out, and Olivier was in. He watched from the bench as his teammates got goal after goal: Olivier, then Blaise, then Mathieu, then Karim, and then Moussa Sissoko. 5–0!

'What about me?' Antoine wondered. 'I want to join in!'

But when he finally came on, the game was already over. Were France better off without him? When Antoine started their final group game against Ecuador, they drew 0–0.

'Just relax, Grizi,' his teammate Paul Pogba told him. 'You're trying too hard!'

Antoine was usually a pretty chilled-out guy, but this was the World Cup they were talking about! The heroes of 1998 and 2002 had inspired him as a kid, and now he was following in their footsteps.

'I'll relax when we've won the trophy!' he replied.

Antoine was back on the bench for France's Round of 16 match against Nigeria. But with thirty minutes to go, it was still 0–0. Deschamps looked at his substitutes and gave Antoine the sign:

'Get ready – you're coming on!'

From the moment he ran on to the pitch, Antoine changed the game. He linked up brilliantly with Karim and Mathieu, playing quick passes and clever one-twos. Maybe France weren't better off without him, after all. They were getting closer and closer, but they still needed to score…

A corner-kick flew high over Antoine's head, but Paul was there at the back post. *1–0!*

'Finally!' the French players cried out with relief.

Could Antoine make it 2–0? He dribbled down the left wing and shot from the edge of the area, but the Nigeria keeper made an excellent save.

'Noooooo!' Antoine groaned with his hands on his head again. It hadn't been Antoine's lucky World Cup so far.

In the last minute, France doubled their lead, and Antoine played a key part. His run into the six-yard box made Joseph Yobo panic and he ended up scoring an own goal.

'I didn't touch the ball, but that's still MY goal!' Antoine told Mathieu with a cheeky smile.

The goal was given to Yobo, but it had helped Antoine to earn his starting spot back for the quarter-final against Germany. He was delighted when he saw Deschamps's teamsheet. Just like in his France debut three months earlier, it was Karim in the middle, Mathieu Valbuena on the right, and Antoine on the left.

'Let's win this!' their captain Hugo Lloris shouted, clapping his goalkeeper gloves together.

But after thirteen minutes, France were 1–0 down. The nation was relying on their front three to fight back...

Antoine crossed to Mathieu, who chested the ball down and struck it fiercely towards the bottom corner. Manuel Neuer dived down to make a super save, but Karim looked certain to score the rebound. Were France about to equalise? No, because Mats Hummels jumped up bravely to block his shot.

'Keep going, the goal is coming!' Antoine urged his teammates as he ran over to take the corner-kick.

He was full of belief but sadly, so was the German defence. France tried and tried but there was just no way past Neuer. At the final whistle, their tournament was over.

All the French players were devastated, but especially Antoine. He hated losing any football match, so losing a World Cup quarter-final hurt like hell. As his tears fell, he wiped them away with the bottom of his shirt.

'Hey, we did our best,' Paul comforted his friend. 'It didn't work out this time, but this is just the start for us, Grizi. We're going to come back bigger and stronger for Euro 2016. We'll be unstoppable!'

CHAPTER 18

NEW ADVENTURES AT ATLÉTICO

Antoine returned to Spain but this time, he didn't return to Real Sociedad. Instead, he was off on an exciting new adventure.

'I arrived here as a boy and I leave as a man,' he told the media in July 2014. 'I want to thank the staff, the supporters and the players for the last ten incredible years.'

Real Sociedad had always believed in Antoine, even when he had been a small, skinny thirteen-year-old boy. He would always be grateful for that, but he felt like he had fully repaid their faith. During his five seasons in the first team, the club had risen all the way from the Spanish Second Division to the Champions League. What a turnaround! Now, however, it was time for a new challenge.

'We'll miss you, Grizi!' the supporters cried out.

But where would Antoine go? After scoring twenty goals for Sociedad and then starring for France at the World Cup, suddenly he had so many options.

'How do you feel about returning to France?' his agent asked him. Monaco were looking for a new superstar to help them compete with PSG.

'Or maybe you'd prefer a move to England?' The top Premier League clubs were also queuing up to buy him: Manchester United, Arsenal, Tottenham, Chelsea...

Antoine shook his head. 'No, I want to stay in Spain for now.'

There was one La Liga club that was top of his list – Atlético Madrid. They had been trying to sign Antoine since 2011. Back then, they had wanted him to replace their star striker Sergio Agüero, who had just signed for Manchester City. That summer, Real Sociedad refused to sell Antoine, but Atlético didn't give up on him. Three years later, they returned with a much bigger offer: £24 million. It was an offer the club had to accept.

'Right, let's do the deal!' Antoine told his agent.

Atlético felt like the perfect place for him to grow as a player. Under Diego Simeone, their amazing Argentinian manager, the club had just beaten Barcelona and Real Madrid to the Spanish League title, and they had reached the Champions League Final too.

'That's my dream!' Antoine exclaimed excitedly.

The team had a deadly defence and a hard-working midfield, but Atlético had just lost their two top goalscorers – Diego Costa and David Villa. Who would replace them? Simeone had already signed the Croatian striker Mario Mandžukić but he also wanted an attacker with speed and skill, who could create chances *and* score goals.

The Atlético manager had made up his mind; that attacker was Antoine. He was a big game player and he had proved it with that acrobatic volley against Lyon and that cool chip against Barcelona.

'You'll be our Messi!' Simeone declared confidently. 'Our Ronaldo!'

'Yes please!' Antoine replied. It was his ideal role. He didn't want to go to Barcelona and sit on the bench behind Messi, Neymar Jr and Luis Suárez. Antoine was twenty-three years old now and ready to take on the responsibility of being a team leader.

From the moment he arrived in Madrid, Antoine was treated like a star. He was Atlético's big signing of the summer, after all. Simeone greeted him with a smile and a firm handshake.

'It's great to have you here. I hope you're ready to win lots of trophies!'

'You bet, boss!'

TV cameras followed Antoine everywhere, even into the medical room. As he lay back in the doctor's chair, he gave a big thumbs-up.

'I'm very excited and happy to join the Atleti family,' he said in his first interview for the club website.

Antoine couldn't wait to start playing football, but

first, their super signing had to be introduced to
the supporters.

'Griezmann! Griezmann! Griezmann!' chanted
6,000 fans as Antoine walked out onto the pitch at
the Vicente Calderón Stadium, wearing the full club
kit. When he raised his arms up to wave, the noise
got even louder. It was an unbelievable feeling.

'This must be what it's like to be Messi!' he
thought to himself.

With his hair slicked back and Number Seven on
the back of his red-and-white-striped shirt, Antoine
looked as stylish as his hero, David Beckham. But did
he have the skills to go with that style?

Of course! After posing for lots of photos, Antoine
entertained the Atleti fans with some keepy-uppies.
Pressure, what pressure? It was like he was back
at the basketball court in Mâcon. With everyone
watching, he went through his full routine:

*Right foot, left foot, right knee, left knee, chest,
head, right shoulder, left shoulder... SELFIE TIME!*

Antoine lifted his phone up high to get as many
people in the photo as possible. 'On the count of

three, everyone say "Atleti". Three, two, one…'

ATLETI!!

The fans loved their new superstar already, but
Antoine would still need to prove himself on the
pitch. What better way to do that than by helping
them to beat their Madrid rivals, Real, in the Spanish
Super Cup?

Before that, however, Antoine had lots of work
to do on the training field. At Atlético, everyone
was expected to chase back and defend, even the
attackers. So, Simeone made sure that all his players
were super-fit. His sessions were a lot more intense
and tiring than the ones at Real Sociedad, but
Antoine was a fast learner when it came to football.
He listened carefully to his manager's instructions
and tried his best to impress him.

'Right, it's time for revenge!' Simeone urged his
team before kick-off at the Bernabeu. Real had beaten
them in the 2014 Champions League Final and the
players wanted payback.

When Antoine came off the bench in the second-
half, the score was still 0–0. 'Great!' he thought to

himself as he ran into position. 'I can become a club hero straight away!'

Sadly, Antoine couldn't create any super-sub chances, but Simeone put him in the Atleti starting line-up for the second leg back at the Vicente Calderón.

'We're gonna win tonight,' he told his strike partner, Mario. 'I can feel it!'

In the second minute of the match, Antoine jumped for a header against Sergio Ramos and managed to flick the ball cleverly through to Mario. He fired a fierce shot into Iker Casillas's bottom corner. *GOAL! 1–0 to Atlético!*

Antoine was delighted with his first assist for his new club. He chased after Mario, pumping his fists at the crowd. 'I told you!' he screamed in his strike partner's ear.

For the next ninety minutes, the players worked really hard to protect their lead. At the final whistle, the Spanish Super Cup was theirs! Antoine had already won his first trophy with Atlético.

'The first of many!' he cheered happily with his new teammates.

CHAPTER 19

THE CHAMPIONS LEAGUE CHALLENGE

Atlético were playing the Greek team Olympiakos in the Champions League. Koke passed to Juanfran and then ran down the right wing, calling for the return pass. As he looked up, he could see Antoine over on the left wing, pointing at the six-yard box. He was about to make his striker's sprint.

'Play it now!' he shouted.

The cross was perfect, and so was Antoine's cool side-foot finish.

Goooooooooooooooooooooaaaaaaaaaaaaaaaaaalllllllllllll llllllllllllll!!!!!!!!!!!!!!!!!!!!

It was Antoine's first goal for Atlético and his first

in the Champions League too. However, there was
no time for a special celebration. His team was losing
3–2 to Olympiakos.

'Cheers, mate!' Antoine said, bumping fists with
Koke as they raced back for the restart.

Despite that early defeat, Atlético still finished top
of their group, ahead of Olympiakos and Juventus.
Next up: Bayer Leverkusen in the Round of 16.

'We're good enough to thrash them!' Antoine
declared confidently.

On top of his two Champions League strikes,
he had also scored fourteen times in La Liga,
including a hat-trick against Athletic Bilbao. Antoine
was on fire! Simeone didn't see him as a tricky
winger anymore; he saw him as a star striker with
clever movement and a lethal left foot. Antoine was
improving all the time in his new role, and he was
hungry for more goals and more glory.

'Well if we don't thrash them, that new hairstyle
of yours is going to look really stupid!' Koke teased
him.

Unfortunately, Atlético lost 1–0 in Germany, and

could only win 1–0 back in Madrid. With the scores tied, it was time for penalties!

'I want to take one,' Antoine told Simeone straight away. His team needed him, and he wasn't going to let them down.

Raúl García missed Atleti's first spot kick, which meant that Antoine really had to score. Pressure, what pressure? After a short run-up, he slammed his shot into the top corner of the net.

'Grizi! Grizi! Grizi!' the fans chanted as he jogged back to the halfway line to join his teammates. Job done!

After Antoine's cool strike, Atlético went on to win the shoot-out. They were through to the Champions League quarter-finals, where they would face... Real Madrid!

'No way, not again!' Koke complained.

'Hey, it's fine,' Antoine argued. 'We beat them in the Super Cup, and we thrashed them 4–0 in La Liga last month. We can do this!'

Why should Atlético be scared of anyone? To win the Champions League, they would have to beat the best teams in Europe. Antoine relished the challenge.

It finished 0–0 in the first leg at the Vicente Calderón, and it was still 0–0 with five minutes to go in the second leg at the Bernabéu. Were Atlético heading for another penalty shoot-out? No, Cristiano dribbled through their defence and set up Javier Hernández to score. *1–0 to Real Madrid!*

'Noooooo!' Antoine groaned on the Atleti bench. He had already been subbed off, so there was nothing more that he could do to help his team. Their 2015 Champions League challenge was over, and soon, so was their La Liga title challenge.

'Next year,' Simeone promised his disappointed players. 'We'll be back, and stronger than ever!'

Until then, Antoine would have to settle for being Atlético's top scorer, and one of the best attackers in Spain. At the La Liga Awards, the 'Team of the Season' featured a front three of:

Ronaldo,

Messi,

and… Antoine!

'Congratulations,' his teammates cheered. 'You're a real superstar now!'

In that moment, Antoine knew that he had made the right choice by joining Atlético. With the support of his amazing manager and teammates, he was getting better and better. And now, after a strong first season, it was time for him to take the next step, and lead his team to Champions League glory...

Antoine scored four goals in six games, as Atlético finished top of their group again. And again, they won on penalties in the Round of 16. This time, Antoine took his team's first spot kick and sent the PSV goalkeeper the wrong way.

'Grizi! Grizi! Grizi!' the fans chanted as he jogged back to the halfway line to join his teammates. Job done! Atlético were through to the Champions League quarter-finals, where they would face... Barcelona.

'Why do we always get the toughest draws?' Koke complained.

'Hey, it's fine,' Antoine argued. 'You guys beat

them in the quarters back in 2014. That was before I arrived, and now we're even better!'

Atlético lost the first leg away at the Nou Camp, but at least Fernando Torres had scored an away goal. That gave them hope for victory back at the Vicente Calderón.

As he waited for kick-off, Antoine took a deep breath and focused on the game ahead. Atleti had to make the most of their home advantage. Up in the stands, their fans never stopped singing, and that noise would spur them on to a special win.

'Come on!' he clapped.

Fernando was suspended, so Antoine was Atlético's main striker. He was always on the move, looking to escape from the Barcelona centre-backs.

'Play it now!'

As the cross came in from the left, Antoine was in lots of space near the edge of the penalty area. He got his head to the ball, but the goalkeeper made a comfortable save.

'Too easy! That needed much more power.'

Antoine was annoyed at himself, but his manager

was full of encouragement. 'Great run, Grizi – keep going!'

From the right wing, Saúl curled another dangerous cross into the box. Antoine was in a perfect position between the Barcelona defenders. He leapt into the air and headed the ball much more powerfully this time.

Goooooooooooooooooooaaaaaaaaaaaaaaaaalllllllllllll llllllllllllll!!!!!!!!!!!!!!!!!!!!

Antoine was so excited that he thought his chest might explode. It was easily one of the most important goals that he had ever scored.

'Yes!' Saúl screamed, throwing his arms around Antoine.

'You hero!' Koke cried out after they had done their cool handshake celebration together.

Would Barcelona bounce back? The trio of Messi, Suárez and Neymar (MSN) attacked again and again, but the Atlético defence was so strong. In the end, it was Antoine who scored the only other goal of the game. He stepped up to the spot and squeezed his penalty into the bottom corner.

Goooooooooooooooooooaaaaaaaaaaaaaaaalllllllllllll llllllllllllll!!!!!!!!!!!!!!!!!!!!!

2–0 to Atlético! Thanks to Antoine, they were
going through to the Champions League semi-finals.
At the final whistle, the players bounced up and
down together in front of the fans. What a night!
The smile stayed on Antoine's face for days. Atleti
were now just two games away from the final.
All they had to do was beat Pep Guardiola's Bayern
Munich.

'Hey, we're good enough to beat anyone!' Antoine
declared confidently.

Saúl's wonder goal was enough to win the home
leg, but out in Germany, Bayern were almost
unbeatable. Even when they scored first, however,
Atlético never gave up. All they needed was one
away goal…

Early in the second half, Antoine nodded the
ball down to Fernando and then ZOOM! He
sprinted past the Bayern defenders to collect the
one-two. What a chance! He was one-on-one with
their sweeper keeper, Manuel Neuer. If he scored,

Atlético would be forty minutes away from a place in the Champions League final. If he missed, the fans would hate him forever.

Pressure, what pressure? Antoine kept his cool and picked his spot perfectly.

Goooooooooooooooooooaaaaaaaaaaaaaaaalllllllllllll llllllllllllll!!!!!!!!!!!!!!!!!!!!

He had done it; he was Atlético's hero and he had led his team all the way back to the Champions League final. Antoine stood in front of the fans and started his new 'Hotline Bling' celebration. But before he could finish, his teammates lifted him high into the air.

'Yes, Grizi!'

'What a hero!'

Antoine couldn't wait for the main event to begin. The 2016 Champions League Final would be a repeat of 2014 – Atlético Madrid vs Real Madrid. Atleti had lost that time, but since then, they had signed a world-class superstar: Antoine. His goals had helped them beat Messi's Barcelona, so why not Ronaldo's Real too?

As he walked out onto the San Siro pitch, Antoine looked as cool as ever. He strolled straight past the glistening trophy and smiled at each of his opponents as he shook their hands. Why shouldn't he be happy? Antoine was playing in his first important final. He was just one more win away from lifting the Champions League trophy.

'Enjoy it, this is your time to shine!' That's what everyone had told him.

Unfortunately, the first goal of the final went to Real, and it was Sergio Ramos who scored it.

'Not again!' the Atleti players thought, but they didn't give up. That wasn't the team's style at all. Instead, they picked themselves up and played on. There was still plenty of time to score.

Antoine, however, was acting like a superstar in a hurry. He took shot after shot from every possible angle. Some flew over, some trickled wide, and some were saved by the goalkeeper – but not one of them went in.

'Take your time!' Simeone urged at half-time.

Things soon looked brighter in the second half.

When Antoine passed the ball forward, Pepe lunged
in and fouled Fernando.

'Penalty!' Antoine cried out.

The referee pointed to the spot straight away.
What a chance for Antoine and Atlético! He placed
the ball down and then took a few steps back.

'It's no big deal,' he told himself. 'It's no different
to taking a penalty in training!'

But Antoine couldn't help getting overexcited. His
strike was a little too hard and a little too high. The
ball crashed back off the crossbar and bounced away.

PENALTY MISSED!

Antoine felt sick with guilt. He had let the club
down at the crucial moment. However, there was
no time to dwell on that mistake. He would have
nightmares about that penalty for weeks to come,
but for now, Atleti were still in the game. And the
only way to make it up to his teammates was to keep
creating chances…

With ten minutes to go, Yannick Carrasco slid in to
score at the back post. *1–1!* Antoine was so relieved
that he raced over to thank his teammate.

'Yes, Yannick – you legend!'

In the end, the 2016 Champions League Final went all the way to penalties. Would Antoine be brave enough to take another one for Atlético after his earlier miss?

Of course he would! His team needed him, and he wasn't going to let them down again. Antoine went first and coolly sent the keeper the wrong way.

'Come on!' he roared. 'We can win this!'

But Atlético's hopes soon faded when Juanfran's penalty hit the post. Ronaldo stepped up and won it for Real.

What a cruel blow! It was a heartbreaking moment for Antoine and his teammates. They lay sprawled out on the grass in shocked silence. After 120 minutes of football and nine nail-biting penalty kicks, they were exhausted and defeated. What was there left to say? Atlético had lost in the Champions League Final… again.

Simeone talked to each of his players and tried his best to lift their spirits.

'Please don't blame yourself,' he told Antoine,

putting a strong arm around his shoulder. 'We win as a team and we lose as a team. You've been brilliant all season, Grizi. You're now one of the best players in the world. I know it hurts but use that pain to lead us back here next year!'

CHAPTER 20

EURO 2016

In the meantime, could Antoine use his Champions League pain to lead France to glory? His country was counting on him. They were the hosts of Euro 2016, and at the previous international tournament held in France, Zidane and co. had won the 1998 World Cup.

'No pressure then!' Paul joked, trying to cheer Antoine up.

They were the leaders of the new-look French team. In attack, there was no Karim, no Mathieu and no Franck. Olivier would be the main striker, with Dimitri Payet on one wing and Antoine on the other, and Paul bursting forward from midfield.

For Antoine, expectations were higher than ever. He had shown for Atlético that he was now one of the best players in the world, up there with Messi and Ronaldo. It was time to prove it for France too, in front of huge home crowds: at the Stade de France in Paris, the Stade Vélodrome in Marseille, and maybe even Lyon's new Parc Olympique Lyonnais, just fifty miles from Antoine's childhood home in Mâcon.

'Grizi, we'll have to win our group if you want to play there!' Paul said, looking at the fixture list. He knew two things that would definitely help make his friend happy again: football and fun.

After training one day, Antoine and Paul put on a skills show for the crowd. They passed the ball back and forth, using all their best flicks and tricks.

'That's more like it, Grizi!'

By the time the tournament started, Antoine's champion spirit had returned and he was back to his usual smiling self. He couldn't wait to represent his country and make the people proud. In front of 75,000 fans, and against Romania, Olivier rolled the ball to Antoine, who passed it back to N'Golo Kanté. Euro 2016 was officially underway!

With Romania sitting deep in defence, France created lots of chances. Olivier headed wide from Dimitri's cross, and then Antoine somehow headed the ball against the post from close range.

'How did I miss that?' he cried up at the sky.

It was another glorious chance missed, and another disappointing day for Antoine. As soon as France were winning, Deschamps decided to take him off.

'Don't worry, we've got plenty more matches ahead of us,' his manager told him.

For the second match against Albania, however, Deschamps dropped Antoine to the subs bench. He had to sit there impatiently as France failed to score again and again.

'Get me out there!' he wanted to scream, but instead, he waited his turn.

When Antoine finally raced onto the pitch, time was running out. A 0–0 draw would be a disastrous result. They simply had to score!

In the penalty area, Antoine never stopped moving.
One second he was at the front post, and the next
he was at the back post. The Albania defenders tried
their best to mark him, but it was impossible! As Adil
Rami crossed the ball into the box with seconds to go,
Antoine was in the perfect position – in between the
two centre-backs. He steered his header down into the
bottom corner. *1–0!*

*Goooooooooooooooooooaaaaaaaaaaaaaaaalllllllllllll
lllllllllllll!!!!!!!!!!!!!!!!!!!*

Antoine had never experienced so many different
emotions at once: passion, pride, frustration, relief
and joy all mixed together.

'Come on!' he roared as his teammates surrounded
him.

It felt so great to finally be France's hero, saving
the day from the subs bench. Antoine had his
confidence back! From that massive moment on, he
became the star of Euro 2016.

In the Round of 16, Antoine powered a brilliant
header past the Republic of Ireland goalkeeper, and
then added a second with his lethal left foot.

Gooooooooooooooooooooaaaaaaaaaaaaaaaaallllllllllll llllllllllllll!!!!!!!!!!!!!!!!!!!!

'You're on fire, Grizi!' Dimitri shouted after kissing his magic boot.

In the quarter-final against Iceland, Antoine made two assists for Paul and Dimitri, and then scored a goal of his own with a cheeky chip.

Gooooooooooooooooooooaaaaaaaaaaaaaaaaallllllllllll llllllllllllll!!!!!!!!!!!!!!!!!!!!

With a wide grin across his face, he did his 'Hotline Bling' dance for the cheering fans. Antoine was really enjoying himself now.

Next up, however, was a big semi-final against Germany – not only the tournament favourites, but also the team that had knocked France out of the 2014 World Cup. *Les Bleus* were going to need Antoine more than ever…

In the last minute of the first half, the referee awarded France a penalty. What a chance to take the lead! But would Antoine be brave enough to take it after his miss in the Champions League final? Of course he would! There were no doubts in his mind. His team needed him, and he wasn't going to let them down. As he calmly put the ball down on the spot, the people of France held their breaths.

Pressure, what pressure? Manuel Neuer dived to his left, and Antoine placed the penalty kick to his right.

Gooooooooooooooooooooaaaaaaaaaaaaaaaalllllllllllll llllllllllllll!!!!!!!!!!!!!!!!!!!!!

Antoine couldn't stop scoring. In the second half, he reacted quickly to poke the ball past Neuer again. 2–0 – game over!

After the full-time whistle, the France players celebrated together in front of their supporters. They had beaten the World Champions, Germany, and they were through to the final of Euro 2016!

Allez Les Bleus! Allez Les Bleus! Allez Les Bleus!

Although it had been a real team effort, Antoine was now France's main man. With six goals, he was the top scorer in the whole tournament. He was also a national hero with a cool new nickname.

'Zizou' had won the World Cup for France in

1998 and eighteen years later, 'Grizou' was about to win Euro 2016 for France.

'No pressure then, Grizou!' Paul joked.

In the Euro 2016 Final, it was France vs Portugal, the country where Antoine's grandparents had grown up. It was also a battle of the superstars – Antoine vs Cristiano Ronaldo. Both players were only one match away from making their international dream come true.

Ronaldo's big day only lasted twenty-five minutes. He hobbled off the pitch in tears with a bad knee injury. Portugal had lost their leader. Surely, the stage was now set for Antoine to win the Euros for France? In the first half, however, he hardly had a chance.

'Come on, Grizou!' Patrice Evra yelled at half-time. 'We need you!'

Antoine was determined to do better in the second half. He dribbled through and shot from the left side of the box, but Rui Patrício made an easy save.

'Unlucky, keep going!' Paul encouraged him.

With thirty minutes to go, Antoine made a clever run between the Portugal defenders to meet Kingsley

Coman's cross. Surely, this was it – the moment that the whole French nation was waiting for.

Antoine jumped up and won the header, but the ball whizzed just over the crossbar. What? How? The fans couldn't believe it, and neither could he.

'Noooooooooooo!' he groaned with his hands on his head. 'How did I miss *that?*'

Antoine had wasted a golden chance to win the final for France. He just had to hope that he would get another opportunity before it was too late...

Unfortunately, it was Portugal's sub striker Eder who scored the winning goal in extra-time. As he watched the ball hit the back of the net, Antoine's shoulders slumped. Was he about to lose another important final? Yes, the final whistle blew, and Portugal were the winners!

Antoine had come so close to achieving his Euro 2016 dream. So close and yet so far. This time, he didn't cry, like he had done when they lost to Germany at the 2014 World Cup. He was older now and more experienced. If he wanted to be France's superstar, he needed to show his teammates that he could be a strong leader.

'This time, we tried and failed,' he comforted them. 'But next time, we're going to succeed!'

Soon, it would be trophy time again. The disappointments only made Antoine more determined than ever.

CHAPTER 21

TROPHY TIME
AT LAST!

Despite France losing in the final, Euro 2016 was
still a massive moment in Antoine's career. 'Grizi'
had become 'Grizou', a national hero and an
international superstar. He won the tournament's
Best Player and Top Goalscorer awards and he even
came in third place for the Ballon d'Or. There were
now only two better footballers in the whole wide
world: Ronaldo and Messi.

'And you're way younger than both of them!' his
proud brother, Theo, reminded him.

After a relaxing holiday back home in Mâcon,
Antoine returned to Madrid, ready to shine again.
Unfortunately, however, the 2016–17 season was

the same old story. Atlético were knocked out in the semi-finals of the Spanish Cup by Messi's Barcelona and then in the semi-finals of the Champions League by Ronaldo's Real Madrid, before finishing third behind both clubs in La Liga.

'I'm fed up with losing to those guys,' Antoine moaned. 'We need to find a way to win something. Anything!'

Antoine had been Atleti's top scorer for three years in a row, but it was clear that he needed more support in attack. Even superstars couldn't get all the goals on their own!

Did the club have enough money to sign a second superstar? If not, Antoine would have to consider his other options. He wouldn't go to Atleti's rivals Barcelona or Real Madrid, but Manchester United were offering him the chance to play in the Premier League with Paul.

'Grizi, you'd love it here!' his friend promised him.

It was tempting, but Antoine wasn't ready to abandon Atlético just yet. He loved the club and he couldn't leave without winning something first. He decided to stay for one more season and if they still hadn't won a trophy, then he would think about moving on.

His Atleti teammates were delighted. 'Great, this is going to be our year,' Saúl announced confidently. 'I can feel it!'

But by December 2017, their season was turning into a disaster. Atlético were already a long way behind Barcelona in the Spanish League and they were out of the Champions League too.

So, Simeone and his players had to switch to Trophy Plan B: the Europa League. Atleti had won it twice before, in 2010 and 2012. It was time for them to complete the hat-trick.

'It won't be easy,' their captain Gabi warned, 'but it's our best shot at winning a trophy!'

Antoine was ready to light up the Europa League, and finally, he had a new star strike partner. Diego Costa was back at Atlético after a successful spell at Chelsea.

'Did you miss me?' he joked on his first day at training.

'Not really,' Koke said with a smile, 'but you and Grizi are a match made in heaven!'

Diego's nickname was 'The Beast' because he was big and strong, and because it was a very bad idea to make him angry. His power, combined with Antoine's pace and skill, would make Atlético better than ever.

Once their Europa League campaign started, Antoine couldn't stop scoring.

He chased after Yannick's through-ball and coolly nutmegged the keeper.

Gooooooooooooooooooooaaaaaaaaaaaaaaaalllllllllllll llllllllllllll!!!!!!!!!!!!!!!!!!!!!

Atlético Madrid 5 Copenhagen 1

He got the ball on the edge of the box and chipped a curling shot into the top corner.

Gooooooooooooooooooooaaaaaaaaaaaaaaaalllllllllllll llllllllllllll!!!!!!!!!!!!!!!!!!!!!

Atlético Madrid 8 Lokomotiv Moscow 1

He pounced on a defender's mistake and dribbled into the penalty area.

Gooooooooooooooooooooaaaaaaaaaaaaaaaalllllllllllll llllllllllllll!!!!!!!!!!!!!!!!!!!!!

Atlético Madrid 2 Sporting Lisbon 1

'Griezmann is far too good for that competition!' some people argued but Antoine wasn't listening. He was fully focused on getting to the Europa League Final, and then winning it. That's all he cared about.

The games were getting tougher and tougher, however. In the semi-finals, Atlético faced Arsenal. In the first leg in London, Antoine's France teammate Alexandre Lacazette opened the scoring for The Gunners but Atlético never gave up. They were the masters of knock-out cup football, and they knew the importance of scoring an away goal…

Antoine chased after a long ball over the top and used his strength to shrug off another France teammate, Laurent Koscielny. He was into the penalty area with just the Arsenal goalkeeper to beat. His first shot was blocked but he scored the rebound.

Goooooooooooooooooooooaaaaaaaaaaaaaaaaaalllllllllllll llllllllllllll!!!!!!!!!!!!!!!!!!!!

What an important strike that would turn out

to be! Antoine ran over to the Atlético fans and did his Fortnite dance for them. Making the letter 'L' on his forehead, he swung his legs from side to side joyfully. Then he turned to celebrate with his teammates.

'Come on!' he roared.

The second leg was played at Atlético's brand-new Wanda Metropolitano Stadium. The atmosphere was electric from start to finish. The club was one win away from another big European final, and the fans cheered them on to victory.

Atleti! Atleti! Atleti!

Just before half-time, Atlético's superstar strike partners scored a great goal together. Antoine got the ball on the right and played a perfect pass into Diego's path. His powerful shot flicked up off the goalkeeper and into the roof of the net.

Atlético Madrid 2 Arsenal 1!

'Yes, Grizi, we did it!' Diego cheered.

That turned out to be the winning goal – Atlético were through to the Europa League Final!

For Antoine, it would be a journey back home.

The match would be against Marseille at the Parc Olympique Lyonnais. That was the new home of Lyon – the club that he had supported as a kid, and the club that had rejected him.

'We've got to win now!' he told his teammates.

It was time for Antoine to shine brightly like a true superstar. So far, he had failed to do so in his two big finals: the 2016 Champions League final with Atlético, and then the Euro 2016 final with France. But now, Antoine was ready to show what a big game player he had become.

As soon as the match kicked off, he was alert and on the move. If there was even half a chance to score, Antoine was going to find it! After twenty minutes, the Marseille goalkeeper played a risky pass to Zambo Anguissa, who let the ball bobble over his foot. In a flash, Gabi gave it to Antoine and this time, he wasn't going to miss.

Goooooooooooooooooooooaaaaaaaaaaaaaaaaaalllllllllllll llllllllllllll!!!!!!!!!!!!!!!!!!!!

Atlético, and Antoine, were off to the perfect start. After a quick Fortnite dance, it was hugs all round.

'Grizi, can you please get a new goal celebration?' Gabi joked. 'That one's rubbish!'

'No way, it's my thing!'

Just after half-time, Antoine was 'Taking the L' again. He passed to Koke and then raced forward for the one-two. Antoine dribbled the ball into the box and at the last second, he lifted it delicately over the diving keeper.

Goooooooooooooooooooaaaaaaaaaaaaaaaalllllllllllll lllllllllllllll!!!!!!!!!!!!!!!!!!!!

'Yes, Grizi!' Koke cried out as they bumped fists.

Two strikes in the final – what a superstar performance!

It was soon game over, and Atlético were the 2018 Europa League winners! At the final whistle, the players laughed and danced and sang.

Campeones, Campeones, Olé! Olé! Olé!

For Antoine, it was triple trophy time. He had also won the Man of the Match award *and* the Best Player of the Tournament prize. The one that mattered most, however, was the team trophy. Having collected his winners' medal, Antoine couldn't wait any longer. He lent forward and gave the cup a quick kiss.

'Hey, I haven't even lifted it yet!' Gabi teased him.

'Sorry, captain!'

Antoine stood with his strike partner Diego as Gabi got ready to raise the trophy high into the Lyon sky. Three, two, one...

Hurraaaaaaaaay!!!!

Atleti! Atleti! Atleti!

CHAPTER 22

WORLD CUP WINNER!

As the Atlético players paraded the Europa League trophy around the pitch in Lyon, there was only one month to go until the 2018 World Cup in Russia.

Antoine counted down the days. He had never been so excited about a tournament in his life. France had come so close to winning Euro 2016 and now, two years later, their team was even better. They had so many talented young players, and especially in attack. Thomas Lemar was twenty-two years old, Ousmane Dembélé was twenty-one, and Kylian Mbappé was only nineteen.

'Man, you guys make me feel so old!' Antoine

moaned as the players arrived for the training camp at Clairefontaine.

'What are you talking about, Grizi?' Paul joked. 'You might be twenty-seven, but you behave like a seven-year-old!'

'Whatever, Piochi. You're just jealous because my goal celebration is better than your silly 'Dab' dance!'

Antoine and Paul were senior players now and two of France's leaders, both on and off the pitch. With their pranks and selfies, they made sure that everyone was smiling and laughing ahead of the main event.

'A happy team is a successful team!' their manager, Deschamps, liked to say.

The fans were just as excited about the World Cup as the players. They couldn't wait to watch Kylian racing down the wing, but they knew that the team's main trophy hopes rested with 'Grizou'. Thanks to his many hairstyles, his cool celebrations and his match-winning goals, Antoine was the most popular man in France.

'Good luck, Grizou!' the supporters shouted as the squad set off for Russia. 'Bring that World Cup trophy home!'

That was Antoine's aim. He was going to lead France all the way to another final and this time, they wouldn't lose.

'Let's do this!' he told Paul.

With a massive month of football ahead of them, France started slowly. In their first match against Australia, they only really got going in the second half. Paul slid a great pass through to Antoine and as he dribbled into the box, a defender tripped him up.

'Penalty!' Antoine cried out.

At first, the referee shook his head but after checking with VAR, he eventually pointed to the spot. Antoine stepped up and...

Gooooooooooooooooooooaaaaaaaaaaaaaaaalllllllllllll llllllllllll!!!!!!!!!!!!!!!!!!!

He was off the mark already!

'Yes, Grizi!' Ousmane cheered, giving Antoine a big hug.

Australia equalised but with ten minutes to go,

Paul's shot bounced down off the crossbar and over the goal line. *2–1!*

'Yes, Piochi!' Antoine screamed, jumping to his feet on the subs bench. What a relief!

France never gave up; that's what made them such a terrific team. Against Peru, Antoine, Paul and Raphaël Varane all missed good chances to score. They didn't panic, though. Paul won the ball in midfield and played it to Olivier. His shot was going in but Kylian made sure. *1–0!*

Kylian ran over to the France fans to do his trademark celebration. Who else loved a goal celebration? Antoine! He stood next to Kylian and copied his moves:

1. Jump to a stop,

2. Fold your arms across your chest,

3. Look as cool as possible.

'I still prefer my Fortnite dance!' Antoine said with a smile.

Kylian's tap-in was enough to send France through to the World Cup Round of 16. So far, so good. Antoine felt like he was still just getting started.

'I'm saving myself for the big games!' he told Paul.

The first of those came against Argentina. The South Americans weren't playing well but, in Messi, they had the best player in the world, plus deadly forwards Ángel Di María and Sergio Agüero.

'Don't you dare underestimate them!' Deschamps told the French players in the dressing room. 'I need you all to stay fully focused until the final whistle.'

Antoine was determined to win the battle of the superstars. When Kylian won a free kick, Antoine grabbed the ball straight away.

'This one's mine,' he told Paul confidently.

'Go for it, Grizi!'

Antoine struck his shot sweetly and it curled up over the Argentina wall and towards the top corner. The keeper hadn't even moved but sadly, the ball bounced back off the crossbar. *So close!*

Five minutes later, Antoine got a second chance to score. Kylian used his electric pace to dribble past three defenders, before being fouled in the box. *Penalty!* Antoine stepped up and…

Goooooooooooooooooooaaaaaaaaaaaaaaaalllllllllllll llllllllllllll!!!!!!!!!!!!!!!!!!!!

As Antoine ran towards the corner flag, he was already making the 'L' sign up above his head. The fans in the stadium copied his Fortnite dance, but Kylian refused.

'No way, I'm not making a fool of myself, mate!'

Antoine carried on working hard for his team, at both ends of the pitch. He chased all the way back to tackle Messi in his own penalty area. The France supporters chanted their hero's nickname:

'Grizou! Grizou! Grizou!'

It was Kylian who stole the show, however. In the second half, he scored two great goals to win the game for France.

'Kyky, what a finish!' Antoine cried out.

He wasn't jealous at all. Winning was a team effort, and France were lucky enough to have a squad full of superstars.

So, who would their hero be, in the World Cup quarter-final against Uruguay? France's attack was taking on the deadliest defence in the tournament:

Diego Godín and José Giménez. Antoine knew them very well because they both played with him at Atlético Madrid.

'Trust me, we'll need to be at our absolute best to beat them,' Antoine told Kylian and Olivier before kick-off.

With time running out in the first half, it was still 0–0. France won a free kick wide on the right and Antoine stood ready to take it. He faked to strike it once, and then *BANG!* The nation held their breath as the ball curled beautifully into the box. Raphaël ran towards it and headed it down into the bottom corner. *1–0!*

'*Allez Les Bleus!*'

Antoine punched the air passionately. He had set up the opening goal and soon he would be scoring one of his own.

When he got the ball on the left wing, Antoine looked up to see who was waiting for one of his dangerous deliveries. But he could only see Kylian, a long way away near the back post…

Suddenly, Antoine had an idea: if everyone was

expecting a cross, why not surprise them with a shot?

BANG! He blasted the ball with plenty of power and it slipped straight through the Uruguay keeper's gloves.

Goooooooooooooooooooaaaaaaaaaaaaaaaaalllllllllllll llllllllllllllll!!!!!!!!!!!!!!!!!!!!

Another big game goal for 'Grizou'! This time, Antoine didn't celebrate with his trademark dance. He decided that it wouldn't be fair to his Uruguayan friends, Diego and José. But inside, the adrenaline was buzzing because France were into the semi-finals!

As the team prepared for their next match, Antoine practised lots and lots of free kicks and corner-kicks. Set-pieces had become a really important weapon at the World Cup. England, for example, were scoring loads of headers, thanks to Kieran Trippier's excellent crosses.

People were calling Trippier 'The New Beckham', but surely that was Antoine? His cross had already created one goal for Raphaël against Uruguay. Could he set up another to help France beat Belgium in the semi-final?

It was a tight game between two brilliant teams. Belgium had the skill of Eden Hazard, the strength of Romelu Lukaku, and the vision of Kevin De Bruyne. France, meanwhile, had the pace of Kylian, the power of Paul and Antoine's ace left foot.

Early in the second half, Antoine curled in a teasing corner and Samuel Umtiti flicked it on. *1–0 to France!*

The centre-back did his own celebration dance and this time, everyone joined in: Antoine, Paul, Raphaël, even Kylian.

'We're nearly there now, lads,' their captain, Hugo, shouted out from goal. 'No silly mistakes, okay? Stay focused!'

France defended magnificently. Antoine ran and ran, making tackles in midfield and then leading his team forward on the counter-attack. Although they didn't quite score a second, they didn't let any goals in either.

At the final whistle, Antoine fell to the floor and

raised his fists to the sky. 'Yessssss!' he cried out joyfully. 'We did it – we're in the World Cup final!'

The big day soon arrived – France vs Luka Modrić's Croatia. There were 78,000 fans watching in the stadium, and millions more back home. Antoine thought about his family, his friends, and his second father, the Real Sociedad scout, Éric Olhats. He wanted to win the World Cup for all of them and he would never get a better chance.

In the seventeenth minute, Antoine won a free kick in a good position for France. What a chance! He curled another incredible cross into the six-yard box and Raphaël made a late run and leap to reach it. He couldn't, but the ball bounced off the head of Antoine's old Atlético teammate, Mario Mandžukić, instead. *Own goal – 1–0 to France!*

'Yes, yes, YES!' Antoine roared as he skidded across the grass on his knees. It was another key assist to add to his collection. They were on their way to World Cup glory…

Twenty minutes later, he got a goal to go with that

assist. When France won a penalty, Antoine stepped up and...

Goooooooooooooooooooaaaaaaaaaaaaaaaaalllllllllllll llllllllllllllllll!!!!!!!!!!!!!!!!!!!!

He had learnt his lesson from that Champions League final; he never lost his cool anymore. Antoine was Mr Calm and Mr Confident. Midway through the second half, he did a couple of keep-uppies in the box and then laid the ball back to Paul. His right-foot shot was blocked, so he tried again with his left. *GOAL – 3–1!*

'Yes, Piochi!' Antoine cheered.

Surely, that was game over? Just in case Croatia were planning an incredible comeback, Kylian made sure with a stunning long-range strike. *4–1!*

'Yes, Kyky!' Antoine screamed.

At last, the full-time whistle blew, and France were the 2018 World Cup winners!

'We did it!' Antoine shouted, hugging his best friend, Paul. 'We're national heroes now!'

It was a night of jubilant celebrations, both there in Russia and back home in France.

Antoine wasn't sure that the smile would ever leave his face. The little football-mad boy from Mâcon had worked so hard for this moment. He had never given up – not even when everyone said he was too small to be a star, and not even when it looked like he would never lift a top trophy.

And now, his ultimate dream had come true. Not only was he a World Cup winner, but he was also the Man of the Match in the World Cup Final, with a goal and two assists. Move over Messi and Ronaldo: Antoine was now the best big game player in the world!

Turn the page for a sneak preview of
another brilliant football story by
Matt and Tom Oldfield. . .

DE GEA

Available now!

CHAPTER 1

THE GREAT WALL

13 January 2019, Wembley Stadium

As they waited in the tunnel, many of the Manchester United players were too excited to stand still. Star striker Marcus Rashford jumped up and down, midfield general Ander Herrera shook out his arms and legs, and captain Ashley Young clapped and cheered.

'This is it, lads – let's get stuck in straight away!'

David, however, stayed as calm and composed as ever. What was there to worry about? If his teammates needed him, United's Number One keeper would be there to save the day.

It had been a bad start to the Premier League

season, both for David and his football club.
However, things were starting to look a lot brighter.
Under new manager Ole Gunnar Solskjær, United
had won six games out of six. They had their
confidence back, but this would be their first big test
– Tottenham away.

For David, that meant the tough task of stopping
Harry Kane, one of the sharpest shooters in the
world. Kane wasn't Tottenham's only amazing
attacker either – they also had Son Heung-min, and
Dele Alli, and Christian Eriksen.

David, however, was determined. Despite a
difficult 2018 World Cup, he was still one of the
greatest goalkeepers in the world. It was time to
prove it. At his best, he was absolutely unbeatable!

'And I'm back to my best now,' he told himself
confidently, as the match kicked off.

In the first half, David didn't have very much to
do. Instead, United were up at the other end of the
pitch, attacking. Paul Pogba played a brilliant pass to
Rashford and he scored past Hugo Lloris. *1–0!*

'Yes!' David yelled, throwing his arms up in the air.

Right, time to really focus. He was about to become a very busy keeper. United were winning at Wembley, and it was David's job to keep it that way.

Kane fired a shot towards the far corner, but he stretched out his long right leg. SAVE!

David loved showing off his fantastic footwork. It was something that he had worked hard on with his first United goalkeeping coach, Eric Steele. Now, it was his superpower, his most dangerous weapon – but by no means his only weapon. When Alli steered a header towards the bottom corner, he dived down and stretched out his long arms just in time. SAVE!

'Who was marking him?' David wondered, but he didn't say it out loud – he wasn't a shouter like his United hero, Peter Schmeichel. Instead, he just got up and prepared himself for his next performance...

Alli burst through the United defence, but David stood up big and tall to block the shot. SAVE!

The Tottenham players couldn't believe it. Was there an invisible wall in front of the goal? No, it was just David, United's Great Wall.

Tottenham had chance after chance, but David made save after save.

Toby Alderweireld kicked the ball early on the volley, but David stretched out his long left leg. SAVE!

Kane's fierce free kick was curling in, but David flew through the air like superman. SAVE!

Not only did David keep the ball out, he managed to catch the ball too! 'Nice one!' the United centre-back Phil Jones said, giving his great goalkeeper a hug.

Tottenham weren't giving up yet, though. Alli got the ball in the penalty area again – would he be third time lucky? No, there was just no way past David. ANOTHER SAVE!

David never let his focus slip, not even for a second. Kane took another shot, but David stretched out his long right leg so far that he did the splits! SAVE!

'Are you okay?' Phil asked him, looking worried. 'That looked painful!'

David nodded calmly. He was fine – no big deal!

In the last minute of the game, Érik Lamela swung a corner into the box, and David rushed out bravely to punch the ball downfield. It was the perfect way to end a perfect display.

As soon as the final whistle blew, David was surrounded by his thankful teammates.

'What a hero!' Ashley screamed in his face.

'We could have played another ninety minutes and they still wouldn't have scored!' Ander added.

'How many saves did you make?' Phil asked. 'I lost count ages ago!'

There were lots more happy hugs to come; with Ole, his manager; with Emilio Alvarez, his goalkeeping coach; and with his friend and teammate, Juan Mata.

Juan looked shocked, as if he'd just watched a magic show. 'I've never seen anything like it!' he said, with a huge smile on his face.

The United fans felt the same way. They clapped and clapped for their super keeper, singing his song over and over again:

He's big, he's brave, he's Spanish Dave,
He makes big saves, he never shaves,
He's flying through the air,
Come and have a shot if you dare!

Amongst those clapping along was Sir Alex Ferguson, the old Manchester United manager who had first brought him to England from Atlético Madrid. Even during his early 'Dodgy Keeper!' days, Sir Alex had been sure that David would one day go on to become one of the best in the world.

José de Gea had always believed in his son too. David had suffered setbacks along the way, but he had bounced back every time. That resilience was a crucial part of being a great goalkeeper. José knew that from experience. Yes, he was a very, very proud dad indeed.

ANTOINE GRIEZMANN HONOURS

Real Sociedad

🏆 Segunda División: 2009–10

Atlético Madrid

🏆 Spanish Super Cup: 2014

🏆 UEFA Europa League: 2017–18

🏆 UEFA Super Cup: 2018

France

🏆 UEFA European Under-19 Championship: 2010

🏆 FIFA World Cup: 2018

Individual

🏆 UEFA European Under-19 Championship Team of the Tournament: 2010

🏆 Onze d'Or French Player of the Year: 2014–15

🏆 UEFA La Liga Team of the Season: 2015–16

🏆 La Liga Best Player: 2016

🏆 French Player of the Year: 2016

🏆 UEFA European Championship Player of the Tournament: 2016

🏆 UEFA European Championship Golden Boot: 2016

🏆 UEFA Team of the Year: 2016

🏆 UEFA Europa League Player of the Season: 2017–18

🏆 FIFA World Cup top assist provider: 2018

🏆 FIFA World Cup Silver Boot: 2018

GRIEZMANN

7 THE FACTS

NAME: ANTOINE GRIEZMANN

DATE OF BIRTH: 21 March 1991

AGE: 27

PLACE OF BIRTH: Mâcon

NATIONALITY: French

BEST FRIEND: Paul Pogba

CURRENT CLUB: Atlético Madrid

POSITION: ST/LW

THE STATS

Height (cm):	174
Club appearances:	444
Club goals:	182
Club trophies:	4
International appearances:	67
International goals:	26
International trophies:	2
Ballon d'Ors:	0

★ ★ ★ **HERO RATING: 89** ★ ★ ★

GREATEST MOMENTS

Type and search the web links to see the magic for yourself!

1 ★ 20 AUGUST 2013, LYON 0–2 REAL SOCIEDAD

https://www.youtube.com/watch?v=q332BYVXGRE

This was the night when Antoine first went from star to superstar. Having helped Sociedad to finish fourth in La Liga, he then got them into the Champions League Group Stage with a win over Lyon. Back in France at the club who had rejected him as a boy, Antoine leapt into the air to score a spectacular scissor-kick.

2 — 13 APRIL 2016, ATLÉTICO MADRID 2–0 BARCELONA

https://www.youtube.com/watch?v=Q5_4ypzAQXQ

Three years on from that scissor-kick, Antoine helped lead Atlético all the way to the Champions League final. Eventually, they lost to Ronaldo's Real Madrid – but before that, they beat Messi's Barcelona. That night, Antoine was the hero, scoring both goals – a header and then a penalty.

3 — 7 JULY 2016, FRANCE 2–0 GERMANY

https://www.youtube.com/watch?v=eQ84ztGmmm8

After a slow start, Antoine became the star of Euro 2016. He scored France's winner against Albania, then two against Republic of Ireland, one against Iceland and then two in this semi-final against the World Champions, Germany. They weren't Antoine's best goals, but he had proved himself at the highest level.

★ 4 16 MAY 2018, MARSEILLE 0–3 ATLÉTICO MADRID

https://www.youtube.com/watch?v=G_dCcR5Q6bs

Antoine's successful summer of 2018 began with the Europa League Final. He had scored four times in the tournament already, and he added two more that night in Lyon. After losing in the Champions League and Euro finals in 2016, at last Antoine showed the world that he was a big game player after all. And there were even greater achievements ahead…

★ 5 15 JULY 2018, FRANCE 4–2 CROATIA

https://www.youtube.com/watch?v=GrsEAvRerTg

Antoine had a wonderful 2018 World Cup, saving his best performance for the final. He set up France's first goal with a fantastic free kick, scored the second from the penalty spot, and then assisted Paul Pogba for the third. Antoine was Man of the Match and made sure that he would stay a national hero forever.

PLAY LIKE YOUR HEROES

ANTOINE GRIEZMANN'S DANGEROUS DELIVERIES

SEE IT HERE

https://www.youtube.com/watch?v=OOpfT0V4KXQ

STEP 1: Practise, practise, practise!

STEP 2: When your team wins a free kick, grab the ball. This is yours; everyone else can back off!

STEP 3: Make sure you send all your biggest players into the box. The more the merrier.

STEP 4: Pick your target – are you aiming for Pete near the penalty spot, or Simon in the six-yard box? Either way, you need to be accurate.

STEP 5: Wait with your hands on your hips. Once the referee blows the whistle, take a couple of short steps towards the ball and then *BANG!*

STEP 6: Put plenty of power and curl on your cross. That way, even the slightest flick might lead to a...

STEP 7: *GOAL!* For you, an assist feels as good as scoring a goal, if not better. I hope you've got a good celebration dance!

TEST YOUR KNOWLEDGE

1. Name at least two of Antoine's childhood football heroes.

2. Which country did Antoine's grandad want him to play for?

3. Which team was Antoine on trial at when he was scouted by Éric Olhats?

4. How old was Antoine when he moved from France to Spain?

5. What was Antoine's first senior trophy?

6. How much did Atlético Madrid pay to sign Antoine in 2014?

7. Which team did Antoine score his first Champions League goal against?

8. What nickname did the French fans give Antoine during Euro 2016?

9. What trophy did Antoine win in May 2018 with Atlético Madrid?

10. What's the name of Antoine's Fortnite dance goal celebration?

11. How many goals has Antoine scored in his last two major international tournaments, Euro 2016 and World Cup 2018?

Answers below. . . No cheating!

1. *Any of the following: David Beckham, Pavel Nedvěd, Zinedine Zidane and Thierry Henry* 2. *Portugal* 3. *Montpellier* 4. *Thirteen years old* 5. *The Spanish Second Division title with Real Sociedad.* 6. *£24 million* 7. *Olympiakos* 8. *'Grizou'* 9. *The Europa League* 10. *Take the L* 11. *10 (6 at Euro 2016 and 4 at World Cup 2018)*

HAVE YOU GOT THEM ALL?

FOOTBALL HEROES

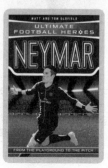